HEART OF THE NATION

HEART OF THE NATION

9-11 AND AMERICA'S CIVIC SPIRIT

JOHN M. BRIDGELAND

For my parents, whose lives of service inspired me; for my family, whose love and support on and after 9-11 kept me going; and for the millions of Americans after 9-11 whose volunteer service helped to heal our nation

CONTENTS

INTRODUCTION

"Take off your shoes and run"

As the director of the President's Domestic Policy Council, on September 11, 2001 I found myself at a hinge point in American history. George W. Bush had been in office for less than 9 months and his administration seemed destined to focus on domestic issues ranging from tax cuts to education reform. But on the day that 19 terrorists hijacked four jetliners and turned them against the American people, a series of events made me realize the course of history was shifting beneath our feet.

One of them came in the White House Mess, the place where aides ate meals, when Secret Service officers feared an aircraft was incoming and told us to run for our lives. Apparently, they thought we had only a few moments to act because one told us to evacuate and another shouted for the women to ditch their high-heeled shoes to outrun the airliner that appeared to be rocketing toward us.

We now know that a plane did not crash into the White House, thanks to the courage of the passengers aboard Flight 93 that brought the plane down in rural Pennsylvania. But that moment and others from that day -- including time in the President's Emergency Operations Center below the White House -- are etched into my memory because 9-11 was more than a tragic attack. It was also a striking cultural moment. For the first time since the War of 1812, when the British burned much of Washington, the White House faced imminent attack. And looking back to that moment we can see that even while terrorists were attacking the ideals of America's free society, the United States had been for years allowing the foundation of those ideals to be hollowed out from within.

On the day the Pentagon was set ablaze and the World Trade Center was demolished, America was on the edge of a decades-long ebb of something the Founding Fathers saw as essential to the maintenance of our liberties -- a civic culture that leads individuals to take on social problems even at great cost to themselves. What was disappearing was a habit of public and community service that had long produced the political leaders the nation needed in crisis, the community leaders capable of pulling others out of the quagmire of poverty, and the volunteers who work to keep alive the connective tissue that ensures our country remains a land of opportunity for all.

For a certain generation, talk of public service evokes memories of a call to action from a young President. On a bitterly cold day in January 1961, John F. Kennedy called on all Americans to keep alive our culture of public service: "Ask not what your country can do for you, ask what you can do for your country." And to the rest of the world, "Ask not what America will do for you, but what together we can do for the freedom of man." Although I was an infant at the time he became President and I would not hear these words until years later, it was this call and Kennedy's presidency that inspired me to enter public service, and it motivated others in the Baby Boomer Generation as well.

Nonetheless, civic participation declined in the decades that followed JFK's inaugural address. Robert Putnam documents in his important book *Bowling Alone*, published in 2000, that in the 1960s, '70s, '80s and '90s many of the activities that define our civic habits -- community volunteering, joining voluntary associations, attending church and public meetings, and charitable giving -- all significantly declined. In the years after JFK's presidency, we lost trust in one another and in our key civic institutions.

Putnam, who was at JFK's inaugural and who felt that the President had personally spoken to him, later explained how disappointing this collapse had been. "Although it felt at the moment like a dawn of a new Athenian renaissance in America, that we were going to be terrific citizens," he said, "it turns out that now in retrospect, half a century later, we can see that that was actually near the zenith of a period of American citizenship . . . a torch had been passed . . . to our generation . . . and then we blew it."

The loss of what Putnam calls "social capital" is destructive for several reasons. It reduces civic virtue – those habits that encourage people to give back to their communities. But more importantly, this loss is destructive because a free society rises and falls on social capital. A society that has limited government requires an active citizenry to take responsibility for essential social tasks that range from helping individuals in need to ensuring every student has access to a quality education to building a foundation that supports creative pursuits in the arts. Our Republic also depends on citizens being active and vigilant. Such engagement is the only effective way to ensure government remains focused on the tasks required of it and determined to protect the liberties bestowed on us by Providence.

The interest in politics seen with the rise of the Tea Party movement in 2009 and 2010 is one example of how an engaged citizenry can channel its energy in ways that drive public policy debates. Through this populist political movement, millions of Americans are paying more attention than they did before and getting organized to elect leaders who will curb government spending, oppose taxes in various forms, adhere to the original intent of the U.S. Constitution, and reduce the national debt. This movement is spurring voter registration drives. It is producing detailed assessments of policies being drawn up in Washington. And it is staging rallies, producing petitions, and otherwise giving Americans a voice on important topics. Regardless of whether you agree with the policy direction the movement would like to take the country, the Tea Parties are functioning the way a democracy should, by pulling citizens into important political debates of the times and directing their passions toward elections.

The key question for voters who join this or other movements is what type of policies will they support once they become part of the process. My hope is that they will see the value of citizen service in a free society. Conservatives have long been leery of government-supported service initiatives because they can at times be wasteful or take government away from its core functions or, worse, create a culture of dependence on government.

But there is no law of nature that requires service initiatives to do any of those things. Indeed, there is a quiet revolution underway in the service arena that is astounding because it can both focus attention on private responsibility while also giving everyone across the political spectrum new ways to unite behind solutions to common problems. Today, the energy and creativity in service initiatives often comes from individuals and private organizations that find new ways to tackle tough problems. From faith-based organizations to non-profits that have the flexibility to quickly adapt to changing conditions on the ground, these organizations and the individuals who serve through them often drive public policy decisions by demonstrating how best to marshal resources to achieve results.

City Year, a nonprofit organization, is but one example of the many institutions that are changing the face of public compassion. Founded in 1988 by Harvard Law School roommates Michael Brown and Alan Khazei to focus mostly on inner city Boston, the organization is now operating in cities across the country. City Year is at the center of a new strategy to boost high school graduation rates by mobilizing its volunteers to mentor and tutor disadvantaged youth in the "dropout factory" high schools (and their feeder middle schools) where graduating is about a 50/50 proposition. It also rebuilds dilapidated public spaces with volunteers who spend a year in the program. It receives about a third of its funding from government sources (AmeriCorps being the largest) and the rest from private donors, including foundations and corporations. After Hurricane Katrina, City Year demonstrated how quickly private organizations can move in a crisis by setting up a program in Louisiana to help with the recovery not long after the waters had receded and then stayed on to help rebuild the city.

Its response to the storm and to other urban problems, along with other private initiatives across the country in recent years pose a challenge to everyone interested in addressing problems facing our communities. Ignore such private initiatives and government programs will likely be less effective even in moments of crisis when public demands for a government response will compel Congress to react. Or embrace them and accept that doing so will create a dynamic and free-flowing marketplace of compassion that will involve a combination of public and private support.

The notion that liberty comes with a responsibility for one's self and one's society is something the Founders well understood and personally exhibited. George Washington gave nearly 50 years of his life to the service of his country. James Madison spoke of creating a culture of virtue that would encourage a vast number of people not simply to pursue their own selfish interests, but also to voluntarily make personal sacrifices for the benefit of society. His generation understood that such sacrifices and work were necessary to bind the country together, as well as unleash a market of talent and compassion to address social needs and keep society functioning.

In the Declaration of Independence, Thomas Jefferson expressed our right to the pursuit of happiness. But he was not simply referring to the right to pursue personal, momentary pleasure fueled by a culture of material goods. The happiness to which he was referring was the right to build a prosperous life within a strong and vibrant community. The happiness of which he wrote was the public happiness – a collective undertaking – that involved the right to self-government and a component of public and community service that brought with it the contentment of a life well lived.

Interestingly, the latest neuroscience and psychological analysis reveals that the Founders were right to believe that our individual happiness is wrapped up in whether we are engaged in society and performing acts of volunteer service. It seems humans are hardwired for social cooperation and acts of civic concern. We are happiest in deep and fundamental ways when serving others.

Fortunately, 9-11 turned out to be a pivotal point in our history. Moments of tragedy and crisis often provide an impetus for us to rethink our personal and national priorities. And that is what happened in the wake of the most devastating terrorist attacks ever carried out on American soil. Americans from all across the country re-engaged in their civic organizations and found new ways to volunteer.

At first, this re-engagement was directed at specific and pressing needs surrounding the 9-11 attacks. From donating blood to voluntarily working at Ground Zero, Americans from across the land responded to the calls for help. But following the attacks many people also conducted a deep reassessment of what's important for them personally and for us as a nation, as evidenced by an increase in civic participation.

My perch at the White House gave me a unique perspective on this re-engagement and efforts made to ensure that it would not wane as memories of the attacks faded. Specifically, the President asked me to spearhead an initiative he hoped would ingrain in our culture the shift toward citizen service. That effort led to the establishment of the USA Freedom Corps and the creation of avenues for millions of Americans to participate in civil society.

Our propensity to freely help one another has long been part of the American character. Ronald Reagan once noted that volunteer service is like a deep and mighty river that flows through American history. Bill Clinton said that citizen service is the very American idea that we meet our challenges not as isolated individuals, but as members of a community. They were right. Our nation has long relied on volunteer service and it needs now more than ever to keep its sights set high to engage more Americans in service to their communities and country. In the process, we can help ourselves discover the true meaning of the pursuit of happiness.

CHAPTER ONE

9-11

When the first plane exploded into the North Tower of the World Trade Center, I was not in my West Wing office or even in the White House complex. I was in the office of Environmental Protection Agency Administrator Christie Todd Whitman to talk about a contentious six-month review of U.S. climate change policy. The news out of New York reached us through her son, who had just taken a job in Building 7 of the World Trade Center. He called to say there had been an explosion and that he saw a person fall from the Tower to the ground. I knew instantly that this was not an accident.

In 1993, my wife Maureen and then three-year-old daughter Caily were having lunch with a friend in the World Trade Center when a massive bomb detonated in the parking garage below. One of my daughter's first memories was of a loud explosion and shattering glass. My wife dove to the floor, believing that a sniper was shooting at people. Instead, it was an attack by a radical Islamic terrorist organization intent on harming the United States and striking at the foundation of our society by detonating a truck bomb along the foundation of one of the world's tallest buildings. It happened in February 1993, more than eight years earlier, but it was still fresh in my mind because it was only good fortune that my wife and daughter emerged unharmed.

Now, sitting in the room with Whitman along with Tom Gibson, her policy advisor, and Jim Connaughton, the chairman of the White House Council on Environmental Quality, I wondered if it was an act of terrorism. I did not believe what CNN was reporting -- that it was a small plane involved in a tragic collision with a skyscraper. But we continued our meeting anyway until we saw the second plane glide across a television screen in the room and disappear into the South Tower. Gibson, a former military officer, was seemingly stunned by the brazen act. Whitman, talking to no one in particular, stated the unthinkable new reality: "My God, we're under attack."

In times of crisis, sometimes people remember only a blur of random events that occur in meaningless rapid succession. For me, the events in and outside of the White House on 9-11 were more like the teeth on a slowly turning flywheel. I could see each advance set in motion other events that were changing the position of the country. Through the course of the day, I went from realizing that we were now a nation at risk of attack from a foreign power to understanding that our nation would need more than just a military response. We would have to undertake a sustained domestic effort to address the security weaknesses revealed by the attacks.

An early event that changed my perspective came in the car ride back to the White House from the EPA. Connaughton and I were in the back seat of one of those black sedans used by the military to shuttle White House officials to and from their dizzying array of meetings. The Pentagon had not yet been hit. But Jim noted that events were unfolding like a Tom Clancy novel and said, "If New York City is under attack, Washington could be under attack -- they could hit the White House."

For a moment, I wondered if we should return to my West Wing office. I remember realizing that this is what it is like to live with the threat of attack to your country. Having just read David McCullough's *John Adams* and re-read Howard Fast's *The Unvanquished* about the struggles of George Washington during the American Revolution, I thought of Adams, Washington, and other revolutionaries who served during a time when cities on the eastern seaboard -- Boston, Brooklyn, and Brunswick – were under attack.

I returned to a surprisingly calm White House, except for one senior counter-terrorism aide who was rushing into the West Wing's Situation Room to join Richard Clarke, the top counter-terrorism official. When I entered my second floor office at around 9:30 a.m., John DiIulio, the head of the White House Office of Faith-Based and Community Initiatives, and his deputy, David Kuo, were waiting for me. They had come to talk about meetings that had been previously scheduled with the President. Upon the President's return from the Emma E. Booker Elementary School in

Sarasota, Florida, we had a full day scheduled with him – a meeting with Catholic Hispanic leaders, another meeting with Muslim leaders, and a domestic policy briefing I was to lead in the late afternoon in the Oval Office. These events were now obviously canceled. We were becoming a nation at war, but the adjustment had not fully taken place just yet as some of our actions were done out of reflexive adherence to the previously set schedule and we continued to watch events unfold on TV.

My assistant Britt Grant told me that while I as at the EPA my friend and tennis doubles partner Jon Missner had called to tell me that CNN was reporting that planes had struck the Twin Towers. Britt called Susan Ralston, Karl Rove's assistant, who called Karl on the road, who then told Andy Card, who then whispered news of the attacks into the ear of the President during his visit to a second grade class in Sarasota. There were other chains of communication through senior staff to the President that day, but this was one of them.

My instinct was to find Josh Bolten. He had been policy director on the presidential campaign and was now Deputy White House Chief of Staff for Policy and a rock of stability. As I walked down the stairs from the second floor to the first, he was coming upstairs to see me.

"A plane has hit the Pentagon," I said, having just learned that from TV reports. Josh's face dropped. I continued, "I think we should evacuate and work from safer ground." Moments later, sometime between 9:45 and 10:00 a.m., we were instructed by security guards to go to the White

House Mess – the place on the first floor where White House commissioned officers (Assistants to the President, Deputy Assistants, and Special Assistants in that seemingly un-American, class-like order of seniority) ate lunch, and often breakfast and dinner.

I remember thinking how odd it was to be crowded into the tiny, unsecure White House Mess with all of the staff. In the hall outside the White House Mess, I again ran into DiIulio. A brilliant public policy professor at Princeton and the University of Pennsylvania before he joined the White House, on this morning he was talking like a national security staffer. He told me we were living through a "classic terrorism mode of operation" – that a first strike might be followed by a biological or chemical attack and possibly a third act, meaning a radiological attack or "dirty bomb." Such a plan, he said, had been written up and discussed by anti-terrorism experts in recent years. I remember feeling this sense of dread that the attacks on that day were just the first troop movements in a protracted and ill-defined war without a clear battlefield. The continental United States had for almost two hundred years been free from foreign attack. With what DiIulio was outlining, I thought things would never be the same for my generation or my children's.

A short while later, an alarmed police officer came into the White House Mess and instructed us to leave. Another officer outside was receiving the latest communications by wire (apparently alerted that United Airlines Flight 93 was headed toward the White House or U.S. Capitol Building) and commanded us, "Take off your shoes and run as fast as you can." I left my shoes on, but I ran down West Wing Avenue where I parked my car and heard other officers talking about a plane flying toward Washington aiming for the White House. A lot of us started looking up into the sky. I remember picturing a plane crashing through the White House, home to every President except George Washington.

I called my wife from my cell phone to check on her and our three children. Maureen had already heard about the explosion at the World Trade Center from the same friend on Wall Street who had called in 1993 to assure me that Maureen and Caily were okay. We were worried about our daughter Caily's reaction because of her 1993 experience. But Caily's first thought was to worry about me in the White House -- she did not know I was okay because all phones into the White House were jammed and her school did not have my cell phone number. I remember my colleague Nick Calio, the President's top liaison to Congress, calling his wife to tell her to get their son out of Gonzaga, a Catholic college preparatory high school in Washington.

All of these events were turning the wheels inside my head. As a White House official, I never thought I would have to evacuate my office out of safety concerns. That I had been forced to do so was eye opening and made it clear that we were now entering a different position in the world, one where we had to actively think about a kind of threat we had not fully considered in the past and one where we had to work to strengthen the foundation of our country. We could take nothing for granted, not even our safety.

But the events kept coming. A group of us had left the West Wing together and gathered in the Washington office of Daimler Chrysler, a short distance away. There we began to discuss how the government would continue to function. We started by making checklists of things we needed to do and of things various federal departments and agencies should do. One of the President's speechwriters, Matthew Scully, and I started to share ideas about what the President might say to the nation in an evening address. Mike Gerson, the President's top speechwriter, called to discuss the speech.

Then a number of us – including Calio; Larry Lindsay, the President's Economic Advisor; Albert Hawkins, the President's Director of Cabinet Affairs; and Clay Johnson, the President's close friend and Director of Presidential Personnel -- were summoned to the President's Emergency Operations Center below the White House. There we joined Josh Bolten, Condi Rice, Karen Hughes, Mary Matalin and other senior staff -- essential White House officials capable of carrying out the President's decisions in addressing the crisis. We were entering a command center built to protect those who would have to lead the government in the time of nuclear attack. Thousands of planes were still in the air and no one knew what else might come. At some point in this process, the Vice President asked for and received from the President permission to shoot down a commercial airliner if that was necessary to stop another attack.

I have many memories of the command center. I will never forget Vice President Cheney, with his large hands holding a phone and with three separate pads of paper in front of him. Cheney worked with Transportation Secretary Norm Mineta to keep track of, and eventually ground, every airplane in, or flying into, American airspace. I remember Secretary Mineta getting repeated updates from his staff on the number of planes still in American airspace. He would call their numbers out loud to the Vice President. Cheney was surrounded by a dozen senior staff. I was surprised that his wife, Lynne Cheney, was there. She remained calm throughout. We ate sandwiches together. I found the normalcy of that act odd and could not finish my lunch.

Josh Bolten and I started to discuss the federal government's domestic response and found that there were several questions that needed to be answered. Where was Joe Allbaugh, Director of the Federal Emergency Management Agency? What role would FEMA play in concert with other agencies in the federal government? Were the disaster reponse preparations sufficient for acts of terrorism? Was FEMA coordinating effectively with the local responses in New York and the Pentagon and a Pennsylvania town I would later learn was called Shanksville?

At Bolten's direction, I headed over to the Situation Room in the West Wing to grab Gary Edson, Deputy National Security and International Economic Affairs Advisor, and pay a visit to FEMA. Edson and I drew up a list of things that needed to be done and then we linked up with a counter-terrorism expert from Clarke's team, Lisa Gordon-Haggerty, and headed out to FEMA.

Outside the scene was eerie and a little discomforting. Usually, the West Wing parking lot is bustling with staffers. What we found instead was an absence of activity. We were the only ones taking a car anywhere. Outside the gates, the quiet was also disturbing. The streets were empty. The city seemed to collectively be holding its breath to await the next wave of attacks. Our anxiety was fed by reports -- we now know to be false -- relayed by Gary of bombs going off on the National Mall.

The White House, the city of Washington, and the nation as a whole were resetting, taking a moment to size up our situation and respond to it. At FEMA that response was already underway. Joe Allbaugh was not there. He was trapped in Big Sky, Montana, at a previously scheduled conference, and desperately working to get back to Washington. But his staff was a blur of activity.

FEMA officials, led by Chief of Staff Liz DiGregorio, responded to our dozens of questions with detailed answers. They had activated emergency operations to the highest level and had dispatched urban search-and-rescue teams, disaster medical teams, and disaster mortuary teams to New York and the Pentagon. They had deployed mobile emergency communications systems and were creating staging areas on the ground to manage the emergency response. They were also thinking ahead to what they should do to meet recovery needs – such as providing grants to first responders, public assistance grants, temporary housing, crisis counseling, help with funeral expenses, disaster unemployment assistance, and more. They talked about using the U.S. Army Corps of Engineers to support New York City in removing debris. They were also thinking of ways to increase the capacity of local hospitals in New York City -- no one yet knew that the greatest demand, tragically, was for body bags. When we left FEMA to return to the White House, I was carrying with me the Emergency Declaration for the Release of Federal Aid to New York and Washington for the President to sign.

After handing the Emergency Declaration to the Staff Secretary, who controlled all of the paper flow into the President, I went to my West Wing office to check my email. Few inside the White House had a Blackberry then. I found two things. The first was that the entire area around my office was dark and empty. I remember roaming around the second floor of the West Wing, looking for some sign of life, and no one was there on a Tuesday afternoon. The second was a series of emails revealing that I was not as alone as it might seem. One message was from Sue Rusche, a friend of mine who had started an anti-drug program in Georgia. "Oh, John, how horrible this day has been," she wrote. "Just know how many of us are 150 percent behind you and your colleagues and how grateful we are for your . . . faith in our system. We are thinking of you and stand ready to do whatever we can to help." Such signs of support were a hint of things to come and something that acted as a counterweight to the images filling our TV screens.

Throughout the day, we had seen the details of the attacks. American Airlines Flight 11 from Boston to Los Angeles had crashed into the North Tower of the World Trade Center at 8:46:40 a.m., killing all 92 people on board and people in the North Tower. United Airlines Flight 175, also flying from Boston to Los Angeles, had crashed into the South Tower of the World Trade Center at 9:03:11 a.m., killing all 65 people on board and people in the South Tower. American Airlines Flight 77 from Washington, D.C. to Los Angeles hit the Pentagon at 9:37:46 a.m., killing 64 people on board (including Barbara Olson, the wife of my friend Solicitor General Ted Olson) and many civilian and military personnel in the Pentagon. After a heroic struggle to take back the plane from the hijackers, United Airlines Flight 93 had lost 44 people when it crashed into a Pennsylvania field shortly after 10:00 a.m. The plane was about 20 minutes flying time from Washington, D.C. and had been headed for the White House, or the U.S. Capitol Building, just before it crashed. [i]

Mid-afternoon I went downstairs to re-enter the command center. Doing so was, perhaps, the event that made the final turn of the wheel to change forever my role at the White House. As director of the Domestic Policy Council, I had been in charge of driving the President's domestic policy agenda and working with teams of talented people in and out of government to develop solutions to pressing public policy problems, such as education reform in high poverty schools, unleashing the "armies of compassion" to help the poor and needy, and new policies to further integrate Americans with disabilities into their communities and the workplace. Now, that role would include developing solutions to issues and problems only hours before were unthinkable. I returned to the command center to report back to Josh Bolten about the domestic response to the attacks that was then underway and found myself witnessing the many decisions being made on the fly.

That position moved me from the relatively comfortable world of domestic policy to the unknown world of helping to manage domestic consequences – working with Bolten, Edson and officials throughout the Cabinet who were expert at organizing federal emergency assistance, compensating victims, restoring civil aviation, reopening the financial markets, strengthening border and port security, evaluating the issuance of immigration visas, reviewing proposals to keep the airline industry aloft, and supporting the economic revitalization of New York and Washington. Led by a new homeland security council, we would meet in the White House Situation Room twice a day to coordinate efforts across departments and agencies.

It also moved me toward a task of more lasting importance. Previously I had been involved in policy debates, but soon I would find myself at the leading edge of a push to help keep alive a new spirit that was emerging in American culture. Many Americans would respond to the attacks by seeking to strengthen and unite the country through acts of individual volunteer service. For a time, we were all simply Americans and our country needed us to pull together. The attacks changed the mood of the nation and how we viewed our obligations to each other.

But that was still to come. Many Americans were still struggling to compute in their minds what had just occurred and how it would change the country. Late in the day of 9-11, some 12 hours after the first plane hit, I got a glimpse of what Americans would come to see from their government in the weeks ahead. Senior staff gathered around the table in the Roosevelt Room of the White House, a few steps from the Oval Office.

Joe Allbaugh had made it back to Washington aboard a military aircraft and was now meeting with us to plot the way forward. I could feel the pressure on him. He is a man who exudes confidence and strength. At 6 feet 4 inches tall with a flattop haircut and gruff manner, many came to see him as a hard-bitten and driven man. I and other friends came to know him, when he was manager of George W. Bush's presidential campaign, as a man with a warm heart and an ability to make hard decisions without flinching under pressure. He was one of the three most influential people on the campaign, along with Karl Rove and Karen Hughes. And now it was time for him and others to put ideas of what to do next on the table and ultimately onto the administration's agenda.

If Allbaugh ever wondered why he was not offered a position inside the West Wing after the campaign and instead was named director of FEMA, he shouldn't have. He was precisely the man you would want at the helm of FEMA in a crisis. In seeing him at the White House that night, I thought of my father's favorite line from Hamlet: "There is a Divinity that shapes our ends, rough hew them as we may." Allbaugh was in the right place and where the country needed him. He made quick and good decisions at FEMA and also went on morning talk shows where he comforted the nation with his command of facts and clear grasp of the federal response. He conveyed the calm sense of American determination to set things right after an horrific episode. He was the direct opposite of the instant-gratification nation that had come to dominate the public spotlight before the attacks. We did not know it yet, but 9-11 would begin a reassessment of what we valued as individuals and as a nation.

1.

September 11, 2001: in the President's Emergency Operation Center below the White House. Third from left, the author is asked by White House Deputy Chief of Staff Josh Bolten, fifth from left, to go to FEMA to check on the response.

2.

July 17, 2001: Oval Office. In calmer days before September 11, John Dilulio (Faith-Based Czar) and the author brief the President on the Faith-Based Initiative.

CHAPTER TWO

Creation of USA Freedom Corps

"[I]t was as if our entire country looked into a mirror and saw our better selves." There was a moment after the 9-11 attacks, as President George W. Bush captured with this line in the State of the Union Address in 2002, when the nation reached deep inside of itself and found the best elements of humanity. In the days and weeks that followed the attacks, the scene unfolding at Ground Zero certainly demonstrated that spirit. A visitor who made it past the police cordon to get within a few blocks of the rubble pile, would have witnessed a remarkable moment in our history amid the destruction, sudden desolation, and desecration of the heart of an American city.

William Langewiesche was there in the immediate aftermath of the collapse and wrote in his book *American Ground: The Unbuilding of the World Trade Center*, that a "reversal soon occurred by which people began moving toward the disaster rather than away from it. The reaction was largely spontaneous, and it cut across the city's class lines as New Yorkers of all backgrounds tried to respond. A surprising number of stockbrokers, shopkeepers, artists, and others got involved. For the most part, however, it was the workers with hardhats, union cards, and claims to a manual trade. . ."[ii] He went on to write that by nightfall, "the first clattering of generators lit the scene and an all-American outpouring of equipment and supplies began to arrive. . . . Indeed, there were so many donations so soon that the clutter became a problem, hindering the rescue effort, and a trucking operation was set up just to haul the excess away."[iii]

Melanie Kirkpatrick, an editor with The Wall Street Journal at the time, wrote about a spontaneous phenomenon that occurred in the immediate aftermath of the attacks. As they made their way home, New Yorkers were seen praying to themselves as they walked along the streets. Across the city and across the country, houses of worship opened their doors and many, Kirkpatrick wrote, had hand-lettered signs inviting people in.[iv]

One journalist who slipped past police checkpoints on the first Friday after the attacks would tell me years later of what he saw. In the blocks immediately north of the World Trade Center site, hundreds of workers -- many of whom came from across the country to volunteer their time and expertise -- were streaming down to the rubble pile. On side streets that would have otherwise been reserved for cars, food tents were set up and volunteers were handing out burgers, pizza, and all sorts of other things to a steady flow of workers looking to recharge before getting back to work. In the chaotic first days after the attacks, Americans responded to an explicit need by heeding an implicit call to serve.

At the White House, we saw that response in many ways, including in the form of a call -- thousands of calls -- from Americans dialing in to ask how they could lend a hand.

The job of a President in times of crisis is especially difficult. In this case, it required addressing immediate and pressing needs that could determine whether Americans lived or died and whether the terrorists who had launched this war would be prevented from striking again. But it also called for calibrating the nation's response, for dialing in the full force of a free society in ways that would preserve and even strengthen our ideals while also aiding our natural allies on the world stage, including those who lived under the dictatorship of ideas al Qaeda preached.

The President began to meet this challenge by visiting a mosque shortly after the attacks and meeting with Islamic leaders. Both were aimed at demonstrating that he understood that the 19 terrorists who carried out the attacks were not only striking at the United States, they were also seeking to pervert one of the three Abrahamic faiths -- Christianity and Judaism being the other two. He wanted Muslims in America and around the world to know that anger and American government policies would not be directed at them personally. The President also met the challenge of properly calibrating the national response by reaching out to Afghan people oppressed by the ideology preached by al Qaeda and its ally the Taliban.

One of many policies I had the privilege of spearheading after 9-11 was designed to get American children to think about the desperate condition of Afghan children and to reach out to help. That effort would begin in a public way about a month after the attacks, when the President spoke to the March of Dimes Foundation -- an organization founded in 1938 to help children with birth defects, to protect the health of babies, and ultimately to defeat polio. In a Memorandum to the President dated October 10, 2001, I suggested he announce the creation of a new initiative that would be modeled after the original mission of the March of Dimes in Franklin Roosevelt's Administration, as well as raise money to help 10 million Afghan children overcome the terrible effects of 22 years of civil war and years of misrule by the Taliban. At the time, Afghanistan suffered the highest rate in the world of the death of pregnant women and one in five Afghan babies did not survive long enough to see their first birthday.

The President agreed. The effort -- "America's Fund for Afghan Children" -- was launched and schoolchildren all over America, including my own three children, contributed dimes and dollars to buy books, book bags, health kits, coats, blankets and more to help the children of Afghanistan. In addition to significant levels of aid the U.S. Government was providing to Afghanistan, more than $12 million was raised through this private effort, in partnership with the American Red Cross, which provided tens of thousands of Afghan children with critical supplies they had little hope of obtaining otherwise.[v] For me, the importance and the impact of this program were driven home in a personal way when I had the good fortune in 2002 to give the keynote address to 7,000 volunteers at the American Red Cross convention in Phoenix, Arizona. At the event, American Red Cross officials presented me with a banner made by the children of Afghanistan to take back to the White House, thanking the children of America for their compassion. It was a moving expression of love among children from two nations now at war.

On the evening of 9-11, the President spoke from the Oval Office and reinforced the values we share as Americans when he said, "Terrorist attacks can shake the foundations of our biggest buildings, but they cannot touch the foundation of America. These acts shatter steel, but they cannot dent the steel of American resolve.... Today, our nation saw evil, the very worst of human nature, and we responded with the best of America, with the daring of rescue workers, with the caring for strangers and neighbors who came to give blood and help in any way they could."

Within days of the terrorist attacks, President Bush gave several high profile speeches -- one from the Rose Garden and another to a Joint Session of the Congress. Both were aimed at soothing the country and preparing it for the hard work ahead. In those speeches, the President called on Americans to help neighbors in need and continue to support the victims of this tragedy in New York, Pennsylvania, and

Virginia. These remarks were part of a broader strategy taking shape at the White House. They were followed up with specific initiatives, such as the "Liberty Unites" campaign that created a way for people to help those in need at the three sites that had been attacked. There also were efforts by the U.S. Department of Education to link schools in America with schools in countries with predominantly Muslim populations to foster a better understanding of cultures, religions, and the challenges of daily life. Among other things, students wrote letters to their foreign counterparts and shared perspectives on their days in school and what they were learning. These efforts, while wonderful, were not enough.

So in October, the President pulled me aside after I had finished briefing him in the Oval Office on another issue. He wanted to talk to me about something that had been on his mind. As I rose from the couch closest to the President's chair where I had briefed him many times, Bush stood and looked across the room and out the window. It was late in the day. Behind him hung a portrait of George Washington and to his left stood a grandfather clock, which I had heard mark the passing minutes throughout the meeting. Vice President Dick Cheney was there, having sat in on the briefing, and was now also silently standing and waiting for the President. "Bridge," the President said, "I want an initiative that will foster a culture of service, citizenship and responsibility. Get to work."

The West Wing is a bustling place even in the calmest of times. And right then the national security team was working on dislodging al Qaeda from its redoubts in Afghanistan and taking steps to recover from the most devastating terrorist attack ever on American soil.[vi] But I remember the phrase the President used, the tone and inflections in his voice, and the moment in its entirety. He did not want a program or a policy. He did not want a public relations campaign. He wanted something that could change the culture, something that would not just touch thousands of people, as most of the national service programs of the past had done. He wanted something that would enable 280 million Americans to serve their communities and country in meaningful ways during a time of struggle and over their lifetimes.

I had briefed George W. Bush dozens of times. The first was in a car on the way to my first event with him in my hometown of Cincinnati in July 1999. I briefed him during the campaign almost daily on domestic policy issues, occasionally during the Florida recount, and during the transition while we were preparing to stand up a new administration. I briefed him in the Blair House the day before he took the oath of office on executive action that we recommended he take right away. And I briefed him in the Oval Office once or twice a week through his first year as President on issues ranging from education reform and faith-based initiatives to conservation of national parks and the prevention and treatment of substance abuse. I had grown comfortable in these roles.

But I had never felt so much responsibility as when he asked me to figure out the specifics of an initiative that would drive cultural change. This was not simply another government program -- it was an effort to shift American society to address a long-standing problem for the country that had been exposed by an immediate crisis.

In the weeks that followed, I worked in what we called the "policy bubble." We did not want word about the initiative to leak out before we had settled on its details and before the President himself could announce it in the State of the Union Address, so I was limited to discussing it with a handful of senior White House aides and with my trusted and gifted deputy, Stephen Garrison. I knew limiting the number of people I could consult on the project was a risk, something that could hamper the development of productive ideas. But I also knew preserving the ability of the President to pop it on the country also preserved the best chance for getting the initiative off to a running start. A little surprise would help create the buzz and news stories we would need to reach every corner of the country, while also giving Americans a chance to consider the initiative in its entirety rather than one or two aspects they may not like.

After weeks of consideration and research, we had a breakthrough. I was in the Ward Room, a private dining area adjacent to the White House Mess, with White House aides Karen Hughes, Josh Bolten, Mike Gerson, and Marc Sumerlin, the Deputy Economic Policy Advisor. After we kicked around several ideas, I suggested we launch an initiative that would make volunteer service opportunities readily available to Americans who wanted to serve in their local communities, coupled with investments in existing and new national and international service programs that would enable Americans who were willing to make a substantial commitment of time meeting needs at home or abroad. Such an effort would serve as an incubator and clearinghouse for volunteer initiatives. My thought was that the vast majority of Americans would need to have opportunities in their local communities and be able to have information quickly at hand to fulfill their desire to help. I also knew that more Americans would want to join the Peace Corps or its domestic counterpart, AmeriCorps, or would want to serve to protect the homeland in some way as their act of patriotism in a time of crisis.

A White House coordinating council and citizen-friendly volunteer clearinghouse could take advantage of all of these initiatives in two ways. First, it could serve as a point of contact for Americans who wish to volunteer but who are unsure of where to go and could provide volunteer opportunities sorted by zip code and areas of interest, such as mentoring and tutoring, working in soup kitchens, and signing up for Neighborhood Watch. Second, such a coordinated effort at the White House could take a survey of existing initiatives, spot issues that were not being fully addressed, and mobilize resources and people to address important needs. Third, the White House council could propose increased investments in existing programs, such as Peace Corps and AmeriCorps, and in new programs to be developed that could enable citizens to bolster disaster response efforts in their communities. Such a model would allow us to co-ordinate international efforts as well as domestic initiatives that could range from helping communities in need to increasing volunteer security efforts. It would help us increase volunteer service (which Republicans like) and national and international service (which Democrats support). Karen Hughes instantly got it and said, "That's it!"

But, of course, that's when the intense work required to flesh out the idea began. I charged my staff -- namely Stephen Garrison who arrived at the White House every morning at 4:45 a.m. to brief Chief of Staff Andy Card on the news of the day -- to lead an effort to gather information on all existing service programs. I wanted to know what every U.S. President from George Washington onward had said about citizen service and what specific initiatives they proposed. I asked for an analysis of the pitfalls of former service initiatives as I vaguely remembered something about President Nixon's failed efforts to bring various service programs under one roof.

I solicited ideas from my White House and government colleagues in key departments and agencies. John DiIulio, our faith-based czar, was a huge help. As was Steve Goldsmith, former Mayor of Indianapolis, and Les Lenkowsky, who had a vast knowledge of the non-profit sector. They were then the Chairman and CEO, respectively, of the Corporation for National and Community Service, which oversaw domestic national service programs such as the Senior Corps and AmeriCorps. Lloyd Pearson, Acting Director of the Peace Corps, also offered some creative ideas.

To address new national security concerns and the extraordinary appetite of many Americans to want to serve to strengthen the safety of our communities, I asked the President to create a task force to look at ways citizens could volunteer to protect the homeland. I co-convened that task force with Tom Ridge, the new Assistant to the President for Homeland Security, to examine the role of the citizen in protecting the homeland, and his deputies, Admiral Steve Abbott, a Rhodes Scholar and former commander of an entire U.S. Fleet, and Mark Holman who had served as then Governor Ridge's Chief of Staff and was very politically savvy.

After weeks of analysis inside and outside of the task force, and undertaken in between other White House duties, we emerged with the following facts and architecture:

Citizen service was an old subject in America rooted in our founding documents, including the Declaration of Independence. The desire to be altruistic also appeared to be part of our biology -- it served a social need as well as a personal one.

I'll get to the neuroscience in a later chapter, but what we discovered about our history was that citizen service had been a component to the functioning of our society since the early settlers arrived. The Mayflower Compact, for example, was signed in 1620 by the Plymouth colonists (and I would later learn that I was the grandson 12 generations back of three of its signers, John Alden, Edward Fuller and William Mullins). It served as the foundation of the first government in what would later become Massachusetts and called for mutual co-operation of the settlers into a "civil body politic."

George Washington picked up and embodied the spirit of mutual cooperation in the Mayflower Compact by dedicating decades of his life to the service of his country. As one of the richest men in America, he did not need to join the revolutionaries. Indeed, he had much to lose by doing so. But he did join and became the "indispensible man" of the Revolution. He lost many battles, but won key ones that rallied the country. He also, by the moral force of his presence, kept his army focused on its purpose: building a free society.

The clearest example of that was when he put down a possible rebellion by soldiers who had not been paid that might have struck a fatal blow to the early Republic. Standing in front of his men, he defused the "Newburg Conspiracy" with a simple act. He reached into his pocket and pulled out a pair of eyeglasses. "You will forgive me, gentlemen," he said, "for I have grown not only gray but almost blind in the service of my country." For Washington, as he said at a different point in his life in a speech to the New York legislature, "When we assumed the soldier, we did not lay down the citizen."

John Adams echoed that thought when he once said in a letter to Benjamin Rush, the man who brought Adams and Jefferson back together after years of fighting, that "Our obligations to our country never cease but with our lives." Adams, it is often forgotten, probably did more than any other member of the Continental Congress to ensure the Declaration of Independence was adopted.[vii]

In the 1830s, the astute Alexis de Tocqueville wrote in Democracy in America, "Americans of all ages, all stations in life, and all types of disposition are forever forming associations. There are not only commercial and industrial associations in which all take part, but others of a thousand different types -- religious, moral, serious, futile, very general and very limited, immensely large and very minute..... Nothing, in my view, deserves more attention than the intellectual and moral associations in America."[viii] In studying early post-Revolution America, he found a central pillar to the new and free society being constructed in this country: volunteer associations and the power they had to direct the strength of individuals into the service of society.

Just about every President had called for some type of citizen engagement (and I discuss in a later chapter the defining moments in the country's history that relate to such Presidential efforts). In speeches, I joked that the only President who did not issue some type of call to service or make reference to the role of citizens was William Henry Harrison, who gave the longest inaugural address and then died in 1841, just a month into office.[ix] Interestingly, even he spoke eloquently in his inaugural about the centrality of citizens to our democracy -- that powers do not rest with agencies of government, but with the people -- a "breath of theirs having made, as a breath can unmake, change or modify" the Constitution.

The modern national and community service movement emerged from another time of crisis – the Great

Depression – and Presidents then and since have launched significant service initiatives. In 1933, Franklin Roosevelt began an effort that enlisted more than three million unemployed young men over the following decade to work on public lands through the Civilian Conservation Corps. Roosevelt also encouraged every civilian to serve in some manner on the home front during World War II. His call to service prompted rubber and scrap metal drives to support the war effort and volunteer service, mostly by women, in nursing, United Service Organizations and the American Red Cross.

Summoning a new generation into service, John Kennedy started the Peace Corps to enable Americans to serve two years abroad; and Lyndon Johnson created Volunteers in Service to America (VISTA) as part of his "War on Poverty." Richard Nixon enlisted older Americans in service to the country; and Ronald Reagan gave a moving speech in Detroit calling on us, "to restore, in our time, the American spirit of voluntary service, of cooperation, of private and community initiative; a spirit that flows like a deep and mighty river through the history of our nation" and went on to create an Office of Private Sector Initiatives in the White House. George H.W. Bush created an Office of National Service in the White House, with Congress the Commission on National and Community Service that would pilot national service programs, and eventually the Points of Light Foundation outside of government. And Bill Clinton started a domestic counterpart to the Peace Corps called AmeriCorps, which gave mostly young Americans opportunities to serve for one or two years in programs like Teach for America, Habitat for Humanity, Earth Conservation Corps, and City Year.

Service to one another and to the country was in the fiber of Americans – in our social DNA, and we discovered that many Presidents had actively promoted the service ethic. A democracy not only depends on active citizens who understand issues, vote, and keep public officials accountable, but also relies on active volunteers who do most of the work of civil society, meeting needs in compassionate ways that no government bureaucracy is ever equipped to meet.

As we researched the history of citizen service, we also saw how tragedy bred unity. Robert Putnam, the Harvard social scientist and author said, "Once or twice a century, we are offered a chance for civic renewal that doesn't come again." I knew that the attacks of September 11, 2001, much like the attacks on Pearl Harbor 60 years earlier, could awaken the country out of its civic slumber.

Our review of Presidential initiatives and the civic landscape also showed the trends in our civic habits over the previous 60 years. The generation of Americans that endured the Great Depression and fought World War II had well more than its fair share of hardship. But perhaps because of those hardships, the country had its greatest civic participation and strength from the mid-1940s until the mid-1960s. The Greatest Generation not only defeated Nazism and helped rebuild Europe, it also rebuilt this country from the inside community-by-community, block-by-block. That generation volunteered more, joined organizations more, gave more in charitable contributions, attended church, school and community activities more, and were active neighbors helping those in need more than the generations that would come before or after it.[x] Interestingly, during the same period when our civic stocks rose during the post-World War II years, Americans also voted more, entered public service in greater numbers, and had much lower levels of political polarization than we see today. Even the gap between rich and poor was smaller.[xi]

Unfortunately, civic participation declined significantly starting in the 1960s. In a generation, our civic gains from the post-World War II era were wiped out.[xii] But the tragedy of 9-11 offered an opportunity to reverse the damage. The attacks spurred a change in the national mood. Suddenly, flags began appearing on more houses, bumper stickers taking pride in America emerged on more cars, and first responders were America's newest heroes.

A patina of civility and civic interest covered the invisible hand of pursuing our own interests. Even Democrat Senate Minority Leader Tom Daschle and President Bush showed a new camaraderie, embracing each other on national TV on the House Floor at the 2002 State of the Union address. Americans liked it. We were seeing what the country could become.

It was in this environment -- from a significant decline in civic participation to a tragic event that could reawaken our civic spirits -- that we were charged with fostering a culture of service, citizenship and responsibility. The challenge was to make permanent the spirit of service and sacrifice that had emerged after the attacks by supporting institutions that would foster that spirit and provide new outlets for it. What was needed was for the institutions that mattered most in Americans' lives – workplaces, schools, non-profits and places of worship -- to become outlets for citizen service. And for that to happen, we needed government policy to both encourage those institutions to make necessary changes and in some cases actively work to clear obstacles preventing those institutions from reinforcing healthy and vibrant civic participation; we needed to provide resources to expand national and community service opportunities; and we needed to provide easily accessible information on how Americans could help.

Franklin Roosevelt had his Civilian Conservation Corps; John Kennedy his Peace Corps; George H.W. Bush his Points of Light; and Bill Clinton his AmeriCorps. George W. Bush would have his "USA Freedom Corps." We selected the name for three reasons. We wanted a "corps" to signify that this was something you could actually join. We wanted to connect it to something larger and meaningful to the times -- to reinforce that maintaining our freedom requires some sacrifice. And we wanted to tap the patriotism of Americans in support of a movement for service, citizenship and responsibility. I was advocating for Freedom Corps. Karen Hughes wanted USA added to the name, given the soaring patriotism of the times. So it was.

When I briefed White House senior staff in the Roosevelt Room – the place adjacent to the Oval Office where our senior staff meeting was held each morning -- on the proposed USA Freedom Corps, I was nervous. Staff members had been encouraged to grill me with any questions they had and although I had important allies for the initiative and there was a general enthusiasm for the effort, the room was hot with questions.

The biggest objection centered on the idea that Freedom Corps, through some of its programs, would be "paying people to volunteer." Conservatives have long been opposed to that for the simple reasons that paying someone to volunteer takes the "volunteering" away, could easily morph into creating another form of government worker, and is viewed as a waste of government money. Libertarians had a similar objection -- that paid volunteers would be an easy way for the government to delve into tasks it should not be doing in the first place. Others worried that these volunteers may not be sophisticated enough to address pressing problems and that volunteers do not have any real accountability for results.

All of the concerns had to be taken seriously. After all, the aim was to create an effective change agent for the country -- something that would improve and protect our communities as well as individual lives in ways that would strengthen our free society. And there was one surprise.

Clay Johnson, one of the President's closest friends from college, his former Chief of Staff when he had been Governor of Texas, and at the time Director of Presidential

Personnel, did not like the suggestion that the President ask every American to serve, let alone for at least two years over the course of their lives.

Andy Card encouraged me to sit down with Clay and work through his main concern, which was that it was not the President's job to tell people what to do with their time. Even if the President issued a call to service, Clay wondered how we would measure the response. I had a lot of respect for Clay and welcomed the discussion. After two days of a healthy back and forth debate, Clay got on board with the concept of Freedom Corps. I shared with him that service was a fundamental American trait, that Presidents in every century had asked Americans to serve and sacrifice for the country, and that times of crisis particularly bred these calls to action. I shared with him how we were going to put in place new ways to measure volunteering in America. I did not know if he was simply letting the idea go, or if in fact his central objections were addressed by my answers. But thankfully he agreed to let the initiative move forward. It was a case of when one person, who was close to the President, could have derailed an entire initiative had he not gotten on board.

But the initiative was not a done deal yet. I stepped into the Oval Office twice to talk to the President about the USA Freedom Corps, once as an initial brainstorming session and later to prep him on our plan. George W. Bush can be tough to brief because he has a habit of cutting you off, going right to the core of an issue, and asking the difficult questions. Even for initiatives he requested, his central concern usually revolved around this question: Will the proposed idea really work as advertised? Can we actually move the volunteering needle and effect a culture change? And how will it be managed with accountability for measurable results?

I told him that the mission of the Freedom Corps would be to "foster a culture of service, citizenship and responsibility for decades to come." I told him that the initiative had to begin with an enlistment -- a call to service by the President himself. Research had shown that when you ask people to serve, 65 percent of them do so. If you do not explicitly ask, you get only 25 percent of them to do so, although research did not tell us the influence a President might have on getting people to serve.

The President's response was encouraging. It was a quip. "If I don't ask," he said, "I get 25 percent?" I smiled, but soon followed by bringing up the part of the initiative that was at the heart of Clay's objection. I told the President that after looking at the terms of service in Mormon missionary work as well as the Peace Corps -- which both help mint lifelong commitments to service -- we concluded that he should ask Americans to dedicate the equivalent of two years of their lives to public service, some 4,000 hours of service over a lifetime. I told him we would create ways to measure rates of volunteering every year, something that had never been done on an annual basis, understand why people were volunteering and why some were not, and find creative ways to provide incentives to recognize and thank Americans who stepped forward to serve.

To encourage that level of service and make sure that it was channeled in useful ways, I got to the nub of our proposal. The President would repeatedly issue a call to the American people to serve their neighbors and nation and we would enlist iconic Americans with deep reach into the culture -- athletes, entertainers, Hollywood stars, the media, and others -- to help echo that call.

With each call to action, we would refer Americans to a central clearinghouse where they could go to find places to volunteer in their communities. The clearinghouse would help us leverage and increase existing programs and also create the architecture that would allow us to spot unmet needs and create new initiatives to address them. We would do it by creating a new website that would list places to volunteer by zip code and area of interest, building on the great work that organizations such as Network for Good and Volunteer Match had done. We would create records of service where Americans could record their hours and reflections on their service experiences, and create a new President's Volunteer Service Award that organizations could bestow on volunteers who gave significant amounts of their time to serve, including those who met the President's two year call to service.

We would elevate volunteer and national service and give it top billing at the Presidential level by creating a White House office and a new USA Freedom Corps Policy Council equal in stature to the Domestic Policy, Economic Policy and National Security Councils and with an Assistant to the

President initiating policy and reporting directly, and providing regular briefings, to the President.

But would all of this really increase the number of hours and the number of Americans volunteering in their communities, produce meaningful results in addressing public challenges, and increase civic participation?

I told the President that the architecture we were creating would have immediate results, as well as longer-term effects, starting with launching several new initiatives. One of which was Citizen Corps, which would serve as a mechanism for Americans to perform vital homeland security tasks such as working in concert with local authorities to coordinate security and disaster response efforts and keeping watch on possible terrorists targets. We would create a Medical Reserve Corps to provide "surge" capacity -- more well-trained doctors, nurses and other medical professionals on the ground -- to support first responders in the event of an emergency. We would add volunteers to police and fire departments. And our new architecture would enable us to significantly increase many existing programs. For example, Neighborhood Watch would double in size and Community Emergency Response Teams would triple in size.

We would also increase AmeriCorps to 75,000 volunteers (up from 50,000) and ask organizations that receive federal dollars to enlist an additional 75,000 a year as part-time volunteers. I warned him that this would be a challenge with many conservative Republicans, but worth taking on, since it meant thousands of more volunteers for Habitat for

Humanity, Teach for America, YouthBuild, City Year and many community and faith-based organizations that meet needs in ways government never can.

Senior Corps would grow to 600,000 from 500,000 as we liberalized age and other requirements to serve in the program and tap the talents of the Baby Boom Generation. And we would double the size of the Peace Corps to 14,000 over five years, fostering both peace and prosperity in an increasingly dangerous world.

The faith-based initiative, which was brought under the wing of Freedom Corps, would continue to mobilize volunteers, such as more mentors for children of prisoners, and give organizations more capacity to meet the needs of the poor and needy, as we continued to remove discriminatory barriers to government support of faith-based institutions.

The aim here was to reform government policy, leverage existing assets, and increase the number of ways in which Americans could voluntarily work to better their communities. Our initiative would not tell people what to do, but it would increase the number of people who could get involved. And it would make their efforts effective by enlisting local institutions such as schools, churches, other non-profits and employers to figure out where to focus volunteer resources.

The President slapped his knee and clearly loved the plan. He understood that we were marrying two concepts that had previously competed needlessly -- traditional unpaid volunteer service and longer-term, full-time national service. Republicans would embrace more volunteering in the spirit of Ronald Reagan and George H.W. Bush, and Democrats would like the public investments in national and international service programs, some of which were signature initiatives of former Presidents from their party, such as Bill Clinton and John Kennedy.

The President had already made it clear he did not want just a policy initiative. He wanted to reinforce and strengthen the cultural shift the country was seeing. He felt very deeply about this and his personal commitment to service was inbred. The President came from a family that was devoted to public service and which had long understood why citizen service was essential to the functioning of a free society.

His father, George H.W. Bush, had a strong legacy of service that reached far beyond public office. In addition to dedicating decades of his life to serving in Congress, as the U.S. Representative to the United Nations, Director of the CIA, and Vice President and President, George H.W. Bush spent much of his life volunteering his time, energy and money to public causes. That record was evident to anyone who toured his presidential library on the campus of Texas A&M University in College Station. Beyond images of Bush parachuting even at an old age and the descriptions of his service in World War II where he was once shot down while fighting in the Pacific, there is a section dedicated to volunteer service. His most famous call for volunteering came in his inaugural address in 1989: "I have spoken of a thousand points of light, of all the community organizations that are spread like stars through the Nation, doing good. We will work hand in hand, encouraging, sometimes leading, sometimes being led, rewarding. We will work on this in the White House, in the Cabinet agencies. I will go to the people and the programs that are the brighter points of light, and I will ask every member of my government to become involved. The old ideas are new again because they are not old, they are timeless: duty, sacrifice, commitment, and a patriotism that finds its expression in taking part and pitching in."

President George H.W. Bush created the first Office of National Service, which was ably run by Assistant to the President Gregg Petersmeyer, and eventually the Points of Light Foundation, which was charismatically led by Robert Goodwin for years and is powerfully spearheaded by Michelle Nunn now.

President George H.W. Bush also signed into law the first National Service Act under which he established the Commission on National and Community Service that supported pilot programs that became key parts of President Clinton's AmeriCorps. Building on that work, President Clinton made national service a signature priority and in 1993, Congress enacted the National and Community Service Act. The law turned the Commission into the Corporation for National and Community Service, which would oversee programs that reach millions of Americans through service and school-based service-learning initiatives and offer help to defray the costs of education in exchange for a year of national service.

After I presented the proposal to George W. Bush in the Oval Office, he called me out onto the carpet -- in a good way (and there had been occasions where it had been the opposite). I had worked for him long enough to become comfortable in my role at the White House and with that comfort came a certain contentment. "Bridge," he said, "if anyone can do this, you can." Then he shook my hand and gave me that familiar slight bow of the head to reinforce his point. He wanted me to drop what I was doing and instead run the USA Freedom Corps. It is hard to turn down a request from the President, but as I walked out of the Oval Office the enormity of what he was asking for set in. I joked with Josh Bolten as we walked out, "at least the expectations are low. All he wants us to do is change the culture." Domestic policy advisor Margaret Spellings repeated the President's words back to me, "Bridgie, if anyone…" I welcomed the boost.

On November 8, 2001, in an address to the nation at the World Congress Center in Atlanta, President Bush gave a sneak preview of the Freedom Corps, outlining some of the specific ideas that would later emerge in fuller form. He said:

> Many ask, what can I do to help in our fight.
> The answer is simple. All of us can become a
> September the 11th volunteer by making a
> commitment to service in our own
> communities. . . . So you can serve your country
> by tutoring or mentoring a child, comforting the

afflicted, housing those in need of shelter and a home. You can participate in your neighborhood watch or Crimestoppers. You can become a volunteer in a hospital, emergency medical, fire or rescue unit. You can support our troops in the field and, just as importantly, support their families here at home by becoming active in the USO or groups in communities near our military installations. We also will encourage service to country by creating new opportunities within the AmeriCorps and Senior Corps programs for public safety and public health efforts. We will ask state and local officials to create a new modern civil defense service, similar to local volunteer fire departments, to respond to local emergencies when the manpower of governments is stretched thin. We will find ways to train and mobilize more volunteers to help when rescue and health emergencies arise. Americans have a lot to offer, so I've created a task force to develop additional ways people can get directly involved in this war effort, by making our homes and neighborhoods and schools and workplaces safer. And I call on all Americans to serve by bettering our communities and thereby defy and defeat the terrorists.[xiii]

On Tuesday, January 29, 2002, in his State of the Union address, the President announced the initiative and sketched why it was a vital task to undertake. He said that after the United States was attacked, he saw the courage and sacrifice of firefighters charging into a building that would soon collapse, soldiers charging into the battlefield to defeat al Qaeda, and ordinary citizens charging the challenges facing the nation. He pointed out that to be a strong and vibrant nation we needed citizens who would rebuild our communities and work to ensure that all of our people have opportunities to succeed while also spreading our compassion and free ideals across the globe. He said we needed volunteer doctors and first responders to be ready in moments of crisis and transportation and utility workers to be alert in spotting possible terrorists attacks. He called for increasing AmeriCorps and Senior Corps and for doubling the Peace Corps.

His call was for the nation to come together and ensure that we had the strength and national cohesion to face challenges ahead. And he issued a warning. "This time of adversity offers a unique moment of opportunity -- a moment we must seize to change our culture." He said in the Address, "For too long our culture has said 'If it feels good, do it.' Now America is embracing a new ethic and a new creed: 'Let's roll.'" And he closed his call for a new culture of service this way: "Through the gathering momentum of millions of acts of service and decency and kindness, I know we can overcome evil with great good. And we have a great opportunity during this time of war to lead the world toward the values that will bring lasting peace."

After each major point, Congress gave strong applause -- the longest of which came when the President said, "My call tonight is for every American to commit at least two years -- 4,000 hours over the rest of your lifetime -- to the service of your neighbors and your nation." This was President Bush at his best. On the campaign trail and in his early speeches as President, he would often connect most naturally and depart from his prepared remarks when the issue related to compassion. The issue meant a great deal to him, and while never widely publicly recognized, steering the culture onto a more productive path was one of the reasons he ran for high office in the first place.

Mike Gerson, whom I jokingly called "Rumpelstiltsken," because he could take policy initiatives like the Freedom Corps and weave them into golden words, had crafted the speech. And Karen Hughes, who also possesses a talent to boil down complex ideas into simple, understandable and inspirational phrases, proposed the language having to do with the "gathering momentum of millions of acts of service and decency and kindness." She wanted to ensure that everyone understood that this initiative was building on an already growing feeling in the country of service and sacrifice. The President is an active editor and many of the words were his, and having spoken them, for history, they all became his.

When I would later play videos of the great calls to service in the past century -- from FDR's announcement of the Civilian Conservations Corps, and Kennedy's "Ask Not" to Bush's "Call to Service" -- to my class at Harvard's Institute of Politics and to college classes elsewhere, the students responded to each with excitement. They remarked how powerful FDR's call for young, jobless men to work on our public lands was, how elegant Kennedy's inversion, "Ask not" was, and how substantive President Bush's call to service was. Our aim was to build on the successes of past efforts -- the Peace Corps, after all, has served as an inspirational model for 50 years in providing thousands of Americans opportunities to serve abroad. But we needed Freedom Corps to be bigger than 7,000 positions a year and more comprehensive in scope to meet the needs of the times. We intended to provide opportunities for far more Americans to respond to the historic need that 9-11 presented.

The day after the State of the Union, the President announced in Winston Salem, North Carolina in front of 20,000 people that I would become the first Director of the USA Freedom Corps. Winston Salem had a local coalition of leaders working together on a strong emergency-response effort that was a good example of what we were trying to spark across the country with Citizen Corps. I went out the door with Ari Fleischer, the President's unflappable and quick-witted press secretary who was treated like a rock star on the Presidential event trail, to face the White House press corps and explain the more detailed announcement. There was clear enthusiasm for the initiative. Members of the press corps came up to me afterwards and showed their enthusiasm and even offered that they would be writing favorable stories.

They wanted to help the movement, in an act of civic journalism. The major dailies, including the Washington Post, ran front-page stories with photos of the President looking up and smiling with the USA Freedom Corps banner waving in the background. Coverage of the initiative on TV, radio and in newsprint was widespread and would remain so for two years into the initiative, as we rolled out more than 42 specific components of the USA Freedom Corps that connected more and more Americans to opportunities to help and recognized them for their service.

By my side during the entire time was Stephen Garrison, later a graduate of the Harvard Business School and a common sense, street-smart, hard-working young man who paid attention to details and ensured that everything was in place, including the usafreedomcorps.gov website (now called serve.gov under the Obama Administration) and the 1-800-USA-CORP phone system that would enable any American to sign up to serve. Millions did so.

3.

January 29, 2002: Oval Office. The author provides the President the final briefing on the Freedom Corps that will be launched that night in the State of the Union.

4.

January 30, 2002: Winston-Salem, NC. President Bush launches the USA Freedom Corps, the day after his announcement of the initiative in the State of the Union.

5.

January 30, 2002: Winston-Salem, NC. Author (top left leaning into table), Homeland Security Advisor Tom Ridge (center top) and the President (middle right) hear from emergency responders and other volunteers who have formed a Citizen Corps in Winston-Salem.

6.

September 12, 2008: Tinker Air Force Base, Oklahoma. President Bush meets with "Freedom Corps Greeters" outside Air Force One -- Oklahoma Air National Guard Major Daniel Rooney (on right) who supported Gold Star families; Karen Stark who provided aid to soldiers and military families; and County Sheriff Department Captain Joe Castleberry who was part of the emergency response to Hurricane Gustav in Louisiana.

CHAPTER THREE

Philosophy and Science of Happiness

The words echo in our national consciousness even now, more than two centuries after they were drafted into the Declaration of Independence: "We hold these truths to be self-evident, that all men are created equal, that they are endowed by their Creator with certain unalienable Rights, that among these are Life, Liberty, and the pursuit of Happiness."

As millions of Americans responded to the President's call to serve after 9-11, these words periodically reverberated through my thoughts. We were researching how other administrations had tried to create a culture of citizen service and knew that we were racing the clock. A lot of Americans were yielding to the tug to serve because they perceived a great national need after devastating terrorist attacks. But that tug would weaken over time, even as the need for citizen service would not. I kept thinking of Jefferson's beautifully alliterative enumeration of our inalienable rights because it not only served as an argument for why the Revolution was necessary, it also seemed to be a challenge issued to successive generations of Americans. Embedded in it was a call to service.

Today, we are far removed from the debates in which the Founders engaged. But for Jefferson, what he put forward in the Declaration was a precise and layered argument intended to both signal a break from the past and sketch out a blueprint for building a new civil society in America -- a break powerfully illustrated by the recent discovery at the Library of Congress that Jefferson substituted the word "citizens" for "subjects" when describing fellow Americans in the Declaration.[xiv] Many Americans assume that this blueprint merely aimed to protect a simple form of liberty -- the right of individuals to pursue a course in life of their own choosing. And that was, of course, part of its aim. But there seems to be another aim, a broader objective with deeper and more profound consequences. The Declaration of Independence is an argument for self-government, an argument for citizens to be engaged with their government and in the lives of their communities to serve the public interest and to protect the freedoms they are entitled by God to enjoy.

The argument is best captured in the use of the term "the pursuit of Happiness." Happiness is actually a term the Founders deliberated over at length and used frequently not only in their personal correspondence, but in the documents they drafted to frame a new republic. Today, the term is often associated with pleasure or contentment. But in reading the Declaration of Independence, it is hard to conclude that the

Framers were basing a revolution on immediate gratification or personal gain.

Indeed, a running theme in the Declaration is the need for public safety and security -- conditions that engaged citizens must help sustain. The document even links safety and happiness in a single sentence. Jefferson also borrowed part of his phrase "the pursuit of Happiness" from his fellow Virginian George Mason, who had written in his state's Declaration of Rights in May 1776 about the right to "pursuing and obtaining happiness and safety." A plain reading of the Declaration of Independence then can conclude that what Jefferson and the others were arguing for was a tandem view of liberty -- individual freedom made possible by active citizens who take on the responsibility of self-government and work together to create the security necessary for liberty to thrive. In short, if self-rule is the ultimate check against tyranny, it is because an engaged citizenry is an effective bulwark for the preservation of liberty. Political philosopher Michael Oakeshott summarized the tandem view elegantly when he said that men are good enough to make democracy possible, yet bad enough to make it necessary.

The context for such a view is found in the list of grievances the Declaration makes against the King of England. That list focuses on the fact that the king had a long record of preventing Americans from engaging with their own government or enjoying their own rights. The list includes complaints that the king dissolved colonial legislatures and undermined other institutions that reflected the will of the people. He compelled lawmakers to meet in locations where it was difficult to conduct the people's business. And he appointed a series of officials on whom citizens could hardly keep tabs. The king ignored petitions for the passage of legitimate laws, waged violent war against citizens, and suspended English common law in Canada. The king inhibited trade, taxed colonists without representation, and denied them the basic rights of trial by jury. All of these things get at the same point: the king was stopping citizens from attaining the happiness and liberty that comes from governing themselves in accordance with a long-standing set of laws.

In his book *We Hold These Truths: Understanding the Ideas and Ideals of the Constitution*, Mortimer Adler delves into what the Founders meant when they talked about "Happiness." Adler notes the dichotomy between the common meaning of happiness today with an older definition of the term, a definition that burdens the word with responsibility. He writes about the "ancient ethical conception of happiness as a whole life well-lived because it is enriched by the cumulative possession of all the goods that a morally virtuous human being ought to desire."[xv] Adler also notes that happiness is something that we can work together to help one another achieve -- it is a cooperative pursuit, much as service to others is founded on cooperation and helping our neighbors. He writes, "The pursuit of happiness must be cooperative, not competitive. We do not have the right view of it unless we see it as something which men can help one another to achieve -- instead of achieving it by beating our neighbors. This is the deepest lesson we can learn from Aristotle about happiness, and it was, I should think, a lesson which was not lost on the framers of the Declaration of Independence."[xvi] He concludes that Jefferson and other Founders were using the ancient definition of the term when they included happiness in the founding documents.

Adler is not alone in his view of what the Founders meant by the term happiness. U.S. Supreme Court Justice Anthony Kennedy, who was so concerned about the quality of the debate in high schools and colleges after 9-11 that he conceived of a program called "Dialogue on Freedom" to enlist judges and policymakers to remind students of America's core values and ideas, summed up the meaning of happiness well:

> Happiness? In this era, happiness carries with it the connotation of self-pleasure; there is a hedonistic component to the definition now. However, that's not what Jefferson meant, and it's not what the Framers meant. If you read Washington, he uses the term happiness all the time. As did the other members of the generation at the time of the founding. For them, happiness meant that feeling of self-worth and dignity you acquire by contributing to your community and to its civic life. And that's the concept of happiness that we have to tell our young people is still within their grasp.[xvii]

We can debate what Jefferson actually meant by the phrase, "the pursuit of Happiness," but we cannot know for sure what he meant other than to state, as he said, "the common sense of the matter."[xviii] One of the 20th century's finest political scientists, James Q. Wilson, once told me that he believed Jefferson substituted "pursuit of Happiness" for "property" in the Declaration of Independence (John Locke's phrase was "life, liberty and property") because Jefferson did not want to hearken back to a feudal society.

Howard Mumford Jones devotes an entire book to the subject, pointing to philosophers, state constitutions, declarations of rights, court cases, and private letters of the Founders and others of that time to show the wide variety of meanings that have been taken from the phrase.[xix] The pursuit of happiness appears in the Declaration of Independence, but the Continental Congress rejected Madison's attempt to include it as the first amendment to the U.S. Constitution. Madison's amendment stated, "All power is originally vested in, and consequently derived from, the people," including the individual's right "generally of pursuing and obtaining happiness and safety."[xx] Despite the failure to include it in the federal Constitution, a right to happiness, with variations as to language, appears in 41 state constitutions. What seems clear is that the right to pursue happiness was not predominantly about private pleasures in the usual sense we think of today.[xxi]

While happiness certainly included the ability at some point to retire to private life and enjoy the remainder of one's days, it also entailed a component of social responsibility. At a lecture at Hillsdale College on March 31, 2006, David McCullough, author of *John Adams* and *1776*, said, "When [Adams] and others wrote in the Declaration of Independence about 'life, liberty, and the pursuit of Happiness,' what they meant by 'happiness' wasn't longer vacations or more material goods. They were talking about the enlargement of the human experience through the life of the mind and the life of the spirit." This understanding was consistent with the Greeks' notion of "eudaimonia," which related to virtue, excellence and human flourishing.

The Founders also longed to have private happiness outside of public life. Adams wrote in 1773, as the Revolution began to gather steam, "in this situation I should have thought myself the happiest man in the world, if I could have retired to my little hut and forty acres, which my father left me in Braintree, and lived on potatoes and sea-weed for the rest of my life."[xxii] George Washington expressed a similar sense in 1797, two years before his death at Mount Vernon: "I am once more seated under my own Vine and fig tree, and hope to spend the remainder of my days . . . in peaceful retirement, making political pursuits yield to the more rational amusement of cultivating the Earth."[xxiii]

But we found, while studying the history of citizen service at the White House, that it was the public happiness that compelled many of the Founders to create a new form of government dependent upon the participation of citizens in the affairs of community and government. Ben Franklin and

George Mason, for example, had important things to say about promoting public happiness. In 1753, Franklin wrote, "For my own Part, when I am employed in serving others, I do not look upon myself as conferring Favours, but as paying Debts." For Mason, happiness was closely related to civic virtue. He wrote to his children in his will, "I charge them on a father's blessing never to let the motives of private interest or ambition induce them to betray, nor the fear of dangers or of death, deter them from asserting the liberty of the country and endeavoring to transmit to their posterity those sacred rights to which they themselves were born."[xxiv]

In *Thoughts on Government* in 1776, John Adams defined happiness as a virtuous life: "All sober inquirers after truth, ancient and modern, Pagan and Christian, have declared that the happiness of man, as well as his dignity consists in virtue. Confucius, Zoroaster, Socrates, Mahomet, not to mention authorities really sacred, have agreed in this."[xxv] Adams, who said "our duty to serve our country ends but with our lives," drafted the Massachusetts Constitution and included in it a paragraph about the importance of public and private charity, social affection, and the importance of diffusion of wisdom and knowledge.[xxvi] Adams valued public and private charity as the core of a happy life.

In her book, *American Virtues: Thomas Jefferson on the Character of a Free People*, Jean Yarbrough argues that Jefferson did not believe that people should simply go about their business. She quotes Jefferson as saying in 1816, "no man has a 'natural right in opposition to his social duties.'"[xxvii]

Jefferson also viewed service as a sacrifice. He would call the Presidency a "splendid misery" and believed "public service and private misery to be inseparably linked."[xxviii]

The Founders talked often about public virtue through moral action and self-government. Importantly, they placed their faith in the virtue of the citizenry, not of elected officials. Adams in 1776 observed, "There must be a positive Passion for the public good, the public interest, Honour, Power, and Glory, established in the Minds of the People, or there can be no Republican Government, nor any real Liberty. And this public Passion must be Superiour to all private Passions."[xxix] Adams also made the case we wanted to make at Freedom Corps – that the service of citizens to their communities and nation are not just fleeting, volunteer acts that have little impact; they are the bedrock of our democracy – the little platoons of civil society that make our nation function. He once wrote, "Ambition in a Republic, is a great Virtue, for it is nothing more than a Desire, To Serve the Public, to promote the Happiness of the People, to increase the Wealth, the Grandeur, and Prosperity of the Community."[xxx]

Even Adam Smith, often identified as the icon of capitalism and the profit motive, believed that true happiness was found in the virtue of considering and serving others. In his *Theory of Moral Sentiments*, Smith talked about the importance of realizing our membership in a broader community: "In directing all our actions to promote the greatest possible good, in submitting all inferior affections to the desire of the general happiness of mankind, in regarding one's self but as one of the many, whose prosperity was to be pursued no further than it was consistent with, or conducive to that of the whole, consisted the perfection of virtue."[xxxi] In short, Smith believed membership in society was critical to individual identity – "bring him into society, and he is immediately provided with the mirror which he wanted before."[xxxii]

He counseled, "To be amiable and to be meritorious; that is to deserve love and to deserve reward, are the great characters of virtue."[xxxiii] Of generosity he said, "We never are generous except when we in some respect prefer some other person to ourselves, and sacrifice some great and important interest of our own to an equal interest of a friend or of a superior."[xxxiv]

At face value, the discussion in *Moral Sentiments* of thinking larger than oneself would seem to contradict the idea of self-interest implicit in Smith's most famous work, *Wealth of Nations*, and the concept of the invisible hand and self interest guiding the economy. But Smith didn't see a contradiction. He saw his ideas as being interconnected -- that is, virtue comprises both the qualities to succeed in personal life and the qualities to serve the whole. He wrote:

> If in the course of the day we have swerved in
> any respect from the rules which he prescribes
> to us….if through passion or inadvertency we
> have hurt in any respect the interest or
> happiness of our neighbor; if we have neglected
> a plain and proper opportunity of promising

that interest and happiness -- it is this inmate
who in the evening calls us to an account for all
those omissions and violations, and his
reproaches often make us blush inwardly, both
for our folly and inattention to our own
happiness, and for our still greater indifference
and inattention, perhaps, to that of other
people."[xxxv]

Smith, it turns out, is one of the many voices from history
calling on citizens to serve their communities and country.
Smith believed that our responsibility to ourselves was in
effect a responsibility to the whole.

Ben Franklin recorded the point succinctly in his daily
schedule cited in his Autobiography – "The Morning
Question, What Good Shall I Do This Day?" Franklin
wanted to form a "great Number of good Citizens" and
proposed a secret society of young men to nourish virtue and
agree to an oath that, "The most acceptable Service of God is
doing Good to Man."[xxxvi] Franklin became one of the best
examples in early America of an active citizen and
philanthropist. He founded one of the first volunteer fire
departments, co-founded one of the first hospitals, and
founded and spent considerable time supporting the first
public lending library in America. He even came up with the
library's motto, which expressed his own philosophy of active
citizenship – *communiter bona profundere deum est* – to pour forth
benefits for the common good is divine.

These ideas for promoting public happiness were fundamental to the thinking of the men who gave birth to the American Experiment, and are more than just clues as to how we might rescue our bitter public discourse and enhance our own lives today. Two hundred years after the Founding Fathers envisioned the pursuit of public happiness, scientists now tell us that human beings are physiologically built to want to cooperate. They function and feel better when they do. After the tragedy of 9-11, friends, neighbors and colleagues (and even strangers) commented on how the feeling of solidarity in that dark hour caused them to think more about the needs of others. Americans today long for more solidarity and less partisan rancor.

So it was with excitement that I stumbled across a newspaper article in my White House office in July 2002. The article noted that neuroscientists from Emory University had just released a groundbreaking study that highlighted a quality almost unique to human beings -- the desire to cooperate and be altruistic even though that social behavior does not provide immediate rewards or gratification. My speeches became full of references to the latest neuroscience.

A co-investigator of the study, Dr. Gregory S. Berns, stated, "Our study shows, for the first time that social cooperation is intrinsically rewarding to the human brain, even in the face of pressures to the contrary. It suggests that the altruistic drive to cooperate is biologically embedded -- either genetically programmed or acquired through socialization during childhood and adolescence."[xxxvii] Subjects who persisted with the desire to cooperate and help one another did so by restraining the "impulse to defect and achieve immediate gratification."[xxxviii] I asked my staff to get the study and went on to read that Dr. James K. Rilling and others performed MRI scans and found that several regions of the brain linked to reward processing were activated when people cooperated with each other.

We also discovered this study was not an isolated set of findings, but supplemented years of pioneering work in positive psychology dating back to the 1950s and 60s and growing rapidly in the 1990s and in the past few years. Like our Founding Fathers and the ancient Greeks before them, many psychologists hold the belief that happiness is not about momentary pleasure, but about a well-lived, virtuous life.

I wondered whether, since we wanted to make the case for volunteer service and acts of charity, a person's happiness quotient could be increased by deliberate activity. Sonja Lyubjomirsky of the University of California, Riverside and her colleagues Kennon Sheldon and David Schkade wrote in a 2005 article entitled, "Pursuing Happiness: The Architecture of Sustainable Change," that we can influence perhaps as much as 40 percent of our own happiness, with the other 60 percent dependent on genetics and other factors. [xxxix] Lyubjormisrky, Sheldon and Schkade argued that intentional activity is the best way to increase sustained happiness. And, we hoped at Freedom Corps that service to others would become one of the most effective ways to increase happiness. Lyubjormisrky, Sheldon and Schkade wrote:

Individuals who report a greater interest in helping others, an inclination to act in a prosocial manner, …or intentions to perform altruistic or courteous behaviors are more likely to rate themselves as dispositionally happy. We assume that acts of kindness and generosity can boost happiness in a variety of ways. Such acts may foster a charitable perception of others and one's community, an increased sense of cooperation and interdependence, and an awareness of one's good fortune. In addition, people who commit acts of kindness may begin to view themselves as altruistic people, as well as to feel more confident, efficacious, in control, and optimistic about their ability to help. Furthermore, acts of generosity can inspire greater liking by others, along with appreciation, gratitude, and prosocial reciprocity, all of which are valuable in times of stress and need. Finally, kind behaviors may help satisfy a basic human need for relatedness, thereby contributing to increased happiness.[xl]

Their research followed students who performed five acts of kindness per week over the course of six weeks, usually at some cost to themselves, such as donating blood, helping a friend with a paper, visiting an elderly relative, or writing a thank you note to a former professor. In the end, they found that such activities, even over the short-term, could increase well-being.

So it turned out that the Founders were right to believe that greater happiness is attainable through a virtuous, generous life. The neuroscience and history revealed the culture we were trying to help foster at the White House. A 2005 survey distinguished between different forms of happiness in multiple choice questions that were given to participants: happiness through pleasure, happiness through pursuing something with a larger meaning than one's self, and happiness through pursuit of engaging in civil affairs.[xli] Examples of such engaging activities included volunteering in a hospice or a soup kitchen. While more quantitative research could be done, psychologists Martin E.P. Seligman and Tracy A. Steen of the University of Pennsylvania, Nansook Park of the University of Rhode Island and Christopher Peterson of the University of Michigan concluded that pursuit of meaning and pursuit of engagement are stronger individual predictors of life satisfaction than an orientation toward pleasure. Pleasure is still very important, but more as a supplement to meaningful and engaging activities.[xlii]

We found an interesting article by Martin Seligman and others that identified the virtues that yield a happy life: wisdom, courage, justice, temperance and transcendence. A sixth virtue, "humanity," was defined to consist of kind acts and good deeds for others, love and close relationships, and being aware of the motives and feelings of ourselves and others. The virtues associated with the heart -- among them the humanity virtue -- were deemed more important in fulfilling happiness than cerebral virtues such as learning and curiosity.[xliii]

Research also shows the benefits of happiness include more zest for living, better health and a longer life.[xliv] It is interesting that modern research is consistent with ancient philosophers' notions of happiness. Such research reinforces that a life well lived is not about simple contentment -- notions of private pleasure found in daily life -- but focuses on the pursuit of happiness over the course of a lifetime.

People who get outside of themselves and devote their energies to something beyond their personal contentment -- to helping the poor and needy, to delivering better health care or education, or many other noble pursuits -- come to a wonderful realization. Such conduct is not only good for the country, it is good for them individually. Civic virtue, citizen service, serving neighbors and nation, performing acts of compassion and goodness -- call it what you will -- is good medicine for each of us and for a culture preoccupied by selfishness and materialism.

The Founders, having read the works of Aristotle and many others, and having understood what happiness really meant, intended to build such a culture. They laid a foundation for a Republic that ultimately would be built on the pursuit of happiness in the fullest sense. They checked the power of government in such ways that individuals, working together in voluntary associations all over America, could bring citizens together to serve the public good. The final words of the Declaration swelled the chorus of the Union and bound not only the Founders but us together, one to another --"we mutually pledge to one another our lives, our fortunes and our sacred honor."

Despite grand intentions, however, we often fall short. There is abundant evidence around us that we do not always cooperate. For all the altruism wired into our DNA, as Richard Layard in his book *Happiness* so well explains, "a degree of rivalry is wired into our genes" as well.[xlv] Cooperation needs to be fostered and, historically, Presidents have tried to play a fundamental role in awakening what President Abraham Lincoln would call the "better angels of our nature."

7.

September 17, 2002: Oval Office. On "Citizenship Day" and the 215th anniversary of the signing of the U.S. Constitution, President Bush greets historian David McCullough, who generated ideas for the American History, Civics and Service Initiative that was launched that day in the Rose Garden.

CHAPTER FOUR

"Uncle Sam Wants You"

"It is not the critic who counts; not the man who points out how the strong man stumbles, or where the doer of deeds could have done them better. The credit belongs to the man who is actually in the arena . . . . who spends himself in a worthy cause; who at the best knows in the end the triumph of high achievement, and who at the worst, if he fails, at least fails while daring greatly, so that his place shall never be with those cold and timid souls who neither know victory nor defeat."

On April 23, 1910, former President Theodore Roosevelt delivered these memorable lines in a speech at the Sorbonne in Paris, France. They have since echoed through history as a sharp defense of bold and courageous leadership. But they were also intended to be something else. Roosevelt's speech, delivered a little more than a year after he left office and some two years before he would seek a third term in the White House, was a carefully constructed argument on the role of "citizenship" in democracies. TR argued that the virtuousness of average citizens plays a vital role in free societies because "in the long run, success or failure will be conditioned upon the way in which the average man, the average woman, does his or her duty, first in the ordinary, every-day affairs of life, and next in those great occasional cries which call for heroic virtues. The average citizen must be a good citizen if our republics are to succeed." [xlvi]

The fact that humans are wired to cooperate with each other does not mean that they necessarily do so. There is an extensive literature from economists, psychologists, and other scholars on the conditions under which people will cooperate with one another.[xlvii] But the bottom line seems to be this: leadership matters. As TR understood, good citizenship is not an accidental occurrence. It has to be inspired, cultivated, encouraged, and defended against cynics who downplay its importance.

I saw this first hand in working for a President who wanted to build on the compassion and goodness of the American people by enlisting an increasing number of them to serve. As we developed the Freedom Corps, we discovered that throughout our history citizen service has been used to expand and protect the American Experiment in self rule, that many of the debates previous Presidents engaged in over citizenship are relevant and even prescient to debates today. And we found that our early Presidents saw service by active citizens as a way to preserve the Union. They believed that public participation in government and private industry and voluntary association were what distinguished the United

States from other nations. George Washington, for example, stated in his Farewell Address, "The free Constitution, which is the work of your hands, may be sacredly maintained…You should properly estimate the immense value of your national union to your collective and individual happiness."[xlviii] His successor in the presidency, John Adams, talked of the obligations of an educated citizenry in his only Inaugural Address in 1797 in saying that he wished "to patronize every rational effort to encourage schools, colleges, universities, academies, and every institution for propagating knowledge, virtue, and religion among all classes of the people, not only for their benign influence on the happiness of life in all its stages and classes, and of society in all its forms, but as the only means of preserving our Constitution from its natural enemies."[xlix]

Both Washington and James Madison, the fourth President of the United States and father of the Constitution, envisioned a National University in Washington, D.C. that would help bind the Union together through the education of its citizens. Washington donated land for such a university. Madison, in a speech to Congress, called for establishing a "national seminary" to infuse students with "those national feelings, those liberal sentiments, and those congenial manners which contribute cement to our Union."[l] The Founder's dream of creating a university in the district would come somewhat to fruition in 1821, when Congress passed and President James Monroe approved a charter for what later became George Washington University. Baptist missionaries raised funds for the university's first building. More than 70 years later, Congress chartered American University, which also rightly claims it is the embodiment of Washington's national university, creating a healthy competition to educate citizens in our national identity and character. After the Civil War, the federal government supported the creation of Howard University in the District as a vehicle for bringing the benefits of citizenship to former slaves.

Public or government service as an independent, professional pursuit, not just as a component of good citizenship, took root as the Republic matured. As the industrial economy strengthened after the Civil War and the United States emerged as a world power, many Progressives looked to mediating the excesses of the Gilded Age. President Chester A. Arthur took up the call for a civil service (actually an ancient notion borrowed from the Chinese)[li] from his assassinated predecessor James Garfield. In his first message to Congress in 1881, Arthur said, "The avowed purpose of that [civil service] system is to induce educated young men of the country to devote their lives to public employment by assurance that having once entered upon it they need never leave it, and that after voluntary retirement they shall be the recipients of an annual pension."[lii] In 1883, Congress passed the Pendleton Act, marking the beginning of the modern civil service.[liii]

It was not until Theodore and then Franklin Roosevelt, however, that the citizen service movement, as we have come to understand it today, mobilized a large number of individuals to serve their country in a civilian capacity. TR was speaking at the Sorbonne at a time when industrial democracies were reaching a turning point in history -- a moment when powerful industrialists were amassing tremendous reservoirs of wealth that dwarfed fortunes of the past and at a time when the American frontier had largely been tamed. There were still fortunes for up-and-comers to make out West, of course, but the United States was growing introspective about itself and its role in the world. TR stood in the national spotlight at a time when the country was debating the role of citizens in society, which is likely why he drew a line between simple material success and good citizenship.

"The truth is that, after a certain measure of tangible material success or reward has been achieved," he said in his speech at the Sorbonne, "the question of increasing it becomes of constantly less importance compared to the other things that can be done in life. It is a bad thing for a nation to raise and to admire a false standard of success." He went on to say that there can be "no falser standard than that set by the deification of material well-being in and for itself." A man who continues to pile up wealth that far surpasses his and his family's needs without returning a "corresponding benefit to the nation as a whole," he said, is someone who should be "made to feel that, so far from being desirable, he is an unworthy citizen of the community: that he is to be neither admired nor envied; that his right-thinking fellow countrymen put him low in the scale of citizenship."

Teddy Roosevelt would prove to be one of the first Presidents to become known as a conservationist and it is one of the main reasons his bespectacled face is etched into Mount Rushmore. During a period of rapid development across America, he took bold action to put large tracts of private land into federal custody for the enjoyment and use of future generations. His legacy includes creating 150 national forests, 51 federal bird reservations, 4 national games preserves, 5 national parks, 18 national monuments, and more.[liv] He was also a leading supporter of the Boy Scouts of America as an institution that instilled habits of good citizenship and engaged generations of boys in the enjoyment of these natural resources Teddy Roosevelt worked hard to protect.

It was another Roosevelt also committed to conservation of public lands who mobilized millions of citizens in a time of national crisis to serve the country and to save themselves. On March 9, 1933, Franklin Roosevelt called Congress into Emergency Session to authorize, among other things, a "Civilian Conservation Corps" (CCC) to bring together two threatened resources -- young men who were out of work in the midst of the Great Depression and public lands beset by soil erosion and a declining numbers of trees. Roosevelt pushed for the CCC over the objections of skeptics in his Cabinet, such as Secretary of Labor Frances Perkins. Within five weeks, FDR's program had been enacted into law and was enrolling its first members. The CCC's membership would hit 250,000 by its first summer and soon reach approximately 500,000 young unemployed, unmarried men serving in more than 2,500 camps in every state. These men were paid $30 a month, $25 of which had to be sent to their families. Many described their years of rough camp experiences and hard work not as a brutal period, but as among the happiest days of their lives.[lv] These men experienced what scientists are now proving -- that service is fundamental to human happiness.

In 1940, FDR explained his vision for the CCC in a letter to Norman Thomas: "I became the head of the Greater New York Boy Scouts about 1922 or 1923, and saw so much of their excellent camps that I favored some form of state-wide or nation-wide camps which would get every boy in the country into the great outdoors for at least two weeks every year."[lvi] The term of service in the CCC was usually a year or two.

The results of the CCC were impressive. Numerous courthouses, high schools, and national park buildings and roads date back to the CCC. Over the life of the program, from 1933 to 1942, some three billion trees were planted, 97,000 miles of fire roads were built, 3,470 fire towers were erected, and more than 84 million acres of agricultural land (about the equivalent acreage of our National Park System today) received proper drainage systems. In total, more than three million men expended a countless number of man-hours rebuilding the country's infrastructure and their own confidence in the value of hard work.[lvii]

In looking back at the history of the CCC during my time at the White House, I came to see that the Civilian Conservation Corps taught us many things. Presidential leadership in advancing such an initiative is essential to its success, especially when there is internal opposition. Powerful initiatives are born of tragedy and hardship and struggle. Effective initiatives are also based on meeting important and urgent needs, such as employing young men during the Great Depression to do valuable work on public lands. But such initiatives may also be limited by the short-term needs they are trying to meet. The CCC was very successful and popular (Congress even resisted FDR's attempts to cut the program in the late 1930s), but once the immediate need for it disappeared with the United States' entrance into World War II, the CCC was soon disbanded. Today, good programs carry on the legacy of the CCC, such as Sally Prouty's The Corps Network, but not in the size and scope of the original program.

But there are other service programs that have survived over the years, met immediate needs, and have left a mark on our culture. One grew out of the 1960 presidential campaign and was inspired by legislation then being proposed in Congress.[lviii]

After his TV debate with Richard Nixon in October 1960, John F. Kennedy made an impromptu speech to some 10,000 University of Michigan students, faculty and town residents. At around 2 a.m., Kennedy asked the crowd if anyone would be willing to help people living in impoverished countries overcome hunger, disease, and other pressing problems. "How many of you are going to be doctors, are willing to spend your days in Ghana?," he asked. "Technicians or engineers, how many of you are willing to work in the foreign service and spend your lives traveling around the world? On your willingness to do that, not merely to serve one year or two years in the service, but on your willingness to contribute part of your life to this country, I think will depend the answer whether a free society can compete."[lix]

Shortly before the election in November 1960, Kennedy elaborated on his vision for a Peace Corps in a speech at the Cow Palace in San Francisco, by equating the program to a civilian alternative to a military draft. And Kennedy's inaugural address, now the subject of a captivating book by Dick Tofel, *Sounding the Trumpet*, laid a foundation for the Peace Corps -- "To those people in the huts and villages of half the globe struggling to break the bonds of mass misery, we pledge our best efforts to help them help themselves."[lx] JFK summoned a new generation of Americans with his challenge, "Ask not." He issued the big call to service and with Sargent Shriver's leadership created a small, but innovative program to embody it.

Shriver's February 1961 summary report to President Kennedy of his plan to create the Peace Corps envisioned a bold experiment. He wanted to mobilize volunteers not just through government, but also through colleges and universities, non-profit institutions, and other federal agencies. In addition to a corps of teachers, he wanted to mobilize health workers to help eliminate malaria in Africa. Only one part of his vision in the summary report would be fulfilled during his tenure, but the plan was sufficient for the time

Kennedy acted swiftly on his own words from the Inaugural and Shriver's recommendations, signing Executive Order 10924 on March 1, 1961, to create a Peace Corps on a temporary, pilot basis and appointing Shriver to run it.[lxi] The President promised to have 500 or more people in the field by the end of the year, and asked Shriver to make full "use of the resources and talents of private institutions and groups." The President also said the Peace Corps would "only send abroad Americans who are wanted by the host country -- who have a real job to do," disavowing any Cold War motivation. He declared, "Our Peace Corps is not designed as an instrument of diplomacy or propaganda or ideological conflict." He highlighted the satisfaction borne of hardship -- "Life in the Peace Corps will not be easy….but if the life will not be easy, it will be rich and satisfying. For every young American who participates in the Peace Corps -- who works in a foreign land -- will know that he or she is sharing in the great common task of bringing to man that decent way of life which is the foundation of freedom and a condition of peace."[lxii] This is pursuit of happiness through the Peace Corps.

As with many new ideas, there was sharp opposition. Richard Nixon taunted that it would be a refuge for draft dodgers (a later study we would do showed that less than 1 in 5 volunteers joined for this reason during the period when we had a draft).[lxiii] Former President Eisenhower derided it as a "juvenile experiment." To allay some of the concerns, Kennedy set up the Peace Corps as a draft deferment, not a draft exemption.[lxiv] But the controversy continued. Senator Harris Wofford, a Pennsylvania Democrat who helped Sargent Shriver create the Peace Corps and became the first Peace Corps Director in Africa, told me about the early days of the program. He remembers Nixon calling it a "Kiddie Korps" and believes that "had Kennedy not been killed, and the Peace Corps enshrined as a central part of his legacy, it might well have become a matter of controversy in the 1964 election."[lxv] Based on the controversy I witnessed around other national service programs, such as AmeriCorps, I believe it.

President Kennedy made one of the smartest appointments of his presidency by naming Shriver, the man who had married Kennedy's sister Eunice, to direct the Peace Corps. When I later invited Sargent Shriver to lunch in the White House in February 2002 and asked him to tell me how he became involved in the Peace Corps, he quipped, "President Kennedy made me do it. I was happily married, raising a family and had a great business in Chicago that I was excited to run. President Kennedy kept after me until I accepted the job." It reminded me of my initial reluctance to take the challenge of creating something new when President Bush appointed me to run the Freedom Corps.

But Sarge may have been downplaying his excitement. Wofford told me that Shriver had been planning to run for Governor of Illinois and had thrown himself into campaigning for JFK in 1960 in part because he was bored running the Merchandise Mart. Shriver, according to Wofford, jumped at the chance to run the Peace Corps. I found this interesting and authentic. Despite my own reluctance to move out of the West Wing to run Freedom Corps, I was excited to have the opportunity.

Sargent Shriver was passionate about uplifting humanity. He was in this line of work because he believed in it, not for prestige or power or his own aggrandizement. He was unusual in politics. In fact, when President Kennedy tapped him to direct the Peace Corps, Sarge was being touted as a candidate for Governor or Senator of Illinois. Later, he would be considered a viable Vice Presidential candidate by both President Lyndon Johnson and candidate Hubert Humphrey and would eventually run as George McGovern's Vice Presidential running mate in 1972. But, Shriver was willing to take a back seat to the Kennedy clan and stay focused on doing good and did a lot of his work, especially in the early years of the Peace Corps and the last years of the War on Poverty, without much support. Kennedy even opposed him in creating an independent agency for the Peace Corps -- such an agency was only created because LBJ persuaded the President to go along with the idea, and Sarge won Congress over to the idea. Within two years of its creation, there were 10,000 Peace Corps volunteers working in 43 countries -- more than the number of Peace Corps volunteers today.[lxvi]

Graceful in his later years and true to his passion, Shriver went on to join his wife Eunice in spreading to other countries the Special Olympics she had started, and in breaking down barriers and unleashing energy and creativity for generations of Americans with disabilities to participate in community life. Scott Stossel chronicles this period of Shriver's life in his book, *Sarge*, and a wonderful documentary film, *American Idealist*, provides tapes and recordings of his public service.

The Peace Corps was authorized on September 22, 1961, and funded by the Congress. The President first offered the chairmanship of an Advisory Committee for the Peace Corps to former President Herbert Hoover, who turned it down.[lxvii] Perhaps he should have provided some kind of honorary role to one of the two public servants who birthed the idea and had a bill in the Senate -- Senator Hubert Humphrey. By June 1966, more than 15,000 volunteers were serving in countries around the globe. Over the course of its 50-year history, more than 200,000 volunteers served in 139 host countries (there are only 196 countries in the world today).[lxviii] The call to ask what you can do for your country became the most remembered and revered aspect of Kennedy's short-lived presidency.

Though small-scale, the Peace Corps was a symbolic embodiment of that call. While inspirational, the Peace Corps did not -- or has not yet -- fulfilled President Kennedy's vision to have 100,000 Americans serving abroad each year. JFK and Shriver imagined one million Americans working in Asia, Africa and Latin America each decade and the powerful constituency they would be for a more informed foreign policy. Today, the Peace Corps enlists only a little more than 8,600 Americans to serve in 77 countries abroad.[lxix] These levels are barely above levels achieved in the Bush Administration (which were the highest levels in three decades) and are shameful given that the Peace Corps is a powerful idea and the number of applications always outpaces available positions. Right after 9-11, there were 215,000

Americans interested in joining the Peace Corps and less than 7,000 slots funded by Congress.

Nonetheless, the Peace Corps shows us that even a small program can be a powerful symbol in driving cultural change. Part of the power of the Peace Corps lies in the enlistment -- people are asked to give two years of their lives and to leave the comfort of their homes and communities to travel far distances to help people in other countries whom they have never met. These assignments promote a greater consciousness across cultures, religions, and nations. The first independent, nationally representative survey of Returned Peace Corps Volunteers showed that the vast majority believed their service improved an understanding of Americans in the communities they served, U.S. adaptation to globalization and even U.S. national security.

Peace Corps also fosters a lifetime commitment to service, as a report released in 2011 shows. After their service abroad, Returned Peace Corps Volunteers volunteer in the United States at twice the rate of the U.S. population. Sadly, there have been limits to the program's growth, in part because each position costs the federal government about $90,000 over a two-year term. One of the constraints is that the Peace Corps is a government-to-government program that does not take advantage of the hundreds of non-profits that have sprung up since its creation. By partnering with non-profits and deploying volunteers through them, the Peace Corps could mobilize more Americans to serve abroad at a much lower cost to the taxpayer and could more efficiently marry urgent needs on the ground to skilled American volunteers.

After creating the Peace Corps, Kennedy wanted to create a domestic equivalent of it. So in November 1962, he appointed a Cabinet-level committee, headed by his brother and Attorney General Robert F. Kennedy, to review the feasibility of a National Service Corps. Some of the proposals the task force considered envisioned Americans working in migratory labor camps, on Indian reservations, in slum schools and in prisons.[lxx] The task force's ideas never really got off of the ground.[lxxi] After Kennedy's assassination, however, President Johnson picked up on the domestic service corps idea and created Volunteers in Service to America (VISTA) as part of a broader anti-poverty initiative. That initiative came to life in the Economic Opportunity Act of 1964, the first major initiative of Johnson's War on Poverty.

To run VISTA and other programs in the war on poverty through the Office of Economic Opportunity -- such as Head Start, Youth Corps, Upward Bound, and Community Action -- LBJ turned to the man best positioned to run a national service program, Sargent Shriver. But Shriver was a reluctant inductee into the War on Poverty. He resisted Johnson's call to service until 20 minutes before the President announced the appointment to the nation.[lxxii]

The appointment was a tremendous opportunity for a service advocate like Shriver, but it was also a tough political assignment. From the outset and throughout the decades that followed, LBJ's War on Poverty was controversial and led to sharp political debates over federal spending, power, and their proper role in society. To get many pieces of relevant legislation passed, Shriver would have to cash in the political capital he had accumulated creating the Peace Corps. A New York Times reporter at the time described the environment surrounding the creation of the War on Poverty programs in the 1960s:

> The volunteer service program received little attention during the long and angry Congressional debate over the anti-poverty bill. Critics scoffed at other parts of the program -- the Job Corps camps and training centers for young people, the community-action projects, and special aid for needy college students, teenagers, low-income farmers and small businessmen. But not a voice was raised against the volunteer plan, perhaps because the Peace Corps, once the target of Congressional taunts, has become such a success."[lxxiii]

On December 12, 1964, Johnson greeted the first 20 volunteers of VISTA, ranging from an 81 year old psychologist to a 20 year old college student and three married couples who would be deployed to the urban slums of Hartford, Connecticut, rural poor areas of Kentucky, and migrant worker camps in California.[lxxiv] Johnson stated, "It would be their job to guide the young, to comfort the sick, to encourage the downtrodden, to teach the skills which may lead to a more satisfying and more rewarding life…No aspect of the war against poverty will be more important than the work that you do...Your pay will be low, the conditions of your labor will often be difficult. But you will have the satisfaction of leading a great national effort."[lxxv]

By 2008, more than 177,000 volunteers had served through VISTA to help the poor and needy.[lxxvi] VISTA itself could become more effective by establishing much stronger linkages to anti-poverty programs, such as Head Start, Job Corps, Community Development Block Grants, Temporary Assistance for Needy Families, the Compassion Capital Fund we created after 9-11 and other programs with significant reach.

Some see the War on Poverty as a big government failure. Others credit it for lifting more Americans out of poverty in a shorter period than in any time in U.S. history. Regardless of where you stand politically, it should be clear that the War on Poverty did create lasting programs that touched millions of lives and engrained in at least some citizens a culture of citizen service. It also demonstrated a tendency in our system to cut short funding for service programs in times of war. Both the War on Poverty in the 1960s, the Peace Corps itself after the Vietnam War, and initiatives to mobilize the "armies of compassion" from 2001 to 2006 were eclipsed by billions of dollars that were expended on the military.

In our research for the Freedom Corps, we discovered how effective engaging older Americans in service can be. LBJ put out the call and found an enthusiastic bloc of

Americans willing to heed it. He created what became known as "Senior Corps" programs throughout the 1960s that enabled older Americans to mentor disadvantaged youth, help other frailer seniors live independent lives, and serve more general needs in their communities.

In 1973, President Richard Nixon picked up on these ideas and cemented into law many of the Senior Corps programs that LBJ had created. In most of these programs, small stipends for low-income seniors and reimbursement for transportation and supplemental insurance were provided.

On average, Senior Corps programs enlist among the largest numbers of Americans in volunteer service on an annual basis, numbering around 500,000 or more each year.[lxxvii] Senior Corps, too, could be vastly improved, to meet the huge appetite among Baby Boomers to give back by increasing the income threshold to qualify for the program, decreasing the qualifying age, and supporting new models that can increase the number of skilled older Americans deployed to meet the needs of vulnerable populations. A strong partnership with AARP (which has 40 million members and a strong effort to promote volunteering called Create the Good inspired by AARP Founder Ethel Percy Andrus and spearheaded by Barb Quaintance) should be established with Senior Corps programs to meet such targeted needs.[lxxviii]

Throughout the 1960s and 1970s, service programs were created that depended on the vision of government to meet public needs. But in July 1980, Ronald Reagan would accept his party's nomination for President and deliver, in a moving speech, a blueprint that could capture the creativity of the American people in carrying out the duties of citizenship and meeting public needs:

> Isn't it once again time to renew our compact of freedom; to pledge to each other all that is best in our lives; all that gives meaning to them -- for the sake of this, our beloved and blessed land? Together, let us make this a new beginning. Let us make a commitment to care for the needy; to teach our children the values and the virtues handed down to us by our families; to have the courage to defend those values and the willingness to sacrifice for them. Let us pledge to restore, in our time, the American spirit of voluntary service, of cooperation, of private and community initiative; a spirit that flows like a deep and mighty river through the history of our nation.

As President, Reagan sought to increase opportunities for service with private organizations. In 1981, he created the White House Office of Private Sector Initiatives, followed in 1983 by an Advisory Council on Private Sector Initiatives. A task force Reagan set up, headed by former U.S. Chamber of Commerce Chairman C. William Verity, Jr., presented its findings to the President in December 1982. It detailed private initiatives, highlighted state and private programs, and compiled a database of 480 federal programs that could be matched up with private initiatives. It also sparked 42 governors to create similar task forces within their respective states.

In his 1988 speech accepting nomination for President, George H. W. Bush praised volunteer organizations as a "brilliant diversity, spread like stars, like a thousand points of light, in a broad and peaceful sky."[lxxix] President Bush established an Office of National Service in the White House to expand service opportunities and build private sector collaboration through the creation of the Points of Light Foundation. By the end of his Presidency, he had honored more than 1,000 volunteers who had contributed to the life of their communities and country.[lxxx]

President George H.W. Bush also signed the National and Community Service Act in November 1990, which established the Commission for National and Community Service that provided funding to the Points of Light Foundation and gave federal support to volunteer service efforts through programs such as Senior Corps and Learn and Serve America. The Points of Light Foundation became best known for its support of more than 370 "volunteer centers" across the country that connect citizens with volunteer opportunities in local communities. The Commission also gave grants as part of a pilot program that would later become the full-blown program called "AmeriCorps." In exchange for one year of national service, a person would receive a small stipend for living expenses.[lxxxi]

In September 1993, President Bill Clinton signed into law the National and Community Service Trust Act, which built on the Domestic Volunteer Service Act of 1973 and the National and Community Service Act of 1990.[lxxxii] The signature component of the new law was the creation of "AmeriCorps" (although this term does not actually appear in the federal statute) with opportunities for full-time, one-year service terms with stipends to cover costs and educational awards to provide incentives, particularly for young people, to serve their country. The thrust of the new program, in President Clinton's own words in New Orleans on April 30, 1993, was to "revive America's commitment to community and make affordable the cost of a college education for every American."[lxxxiii] He compared his program to the G.I. Bill and the Peace Corps. His director of National Service, Eli Segal, hoped to grow the program to 150,000 participants by 1997. And in September 1994, Clinton swore in 20,000 AmeriCorps participants.[lxxxiv]

But AmeriCorps met stiff resistance. The military worried about the program luring away potential soldiers. Republicans, who won control of Congress in November 1994, worried about the program's cost and attacked the program as "coerced voluntarism" and "gimmickry."[lxxxv] The House even passed a budget – and continues to pass budgets – to eliminate AmeriCorps. Nonetheless, AmeriCorps lived on.

By the time President George W. Bush entered office, AmeriCorps had 50,000 participants and remained a hot button for many in Washington. I had two Senators warn me that the program was about as controversial as what had become known as "Hillary-Care," First Lady Hillary Clinton's unsuccessful health-care initiative. Senator Hillary Clinton was now one of the strongest and most articulate advocates for national service. After President George W. Bush proposed after 9-11 to increase AmeriCorps by 50 percent, House Majority Leader Dick Armey called the proposal "obnoxious" and initially refused to bring any such expansion to the House Floor.

The AmeriCorps experience teaches us a number of things. First, it is possible to create a national service program, even when facing high-profile political opposition. Second, such a program need not be as expensive as the Peace Corps. Paying volunteers was not popular. But providing below poverty level stipends (about $10,000 a year) and offering volunteers assistance in paying college tuition (or paying off student loans) would draw significant numbers of people to serve their country. Third, AmeriCorps showed that funding national service through a broad network of existing non-profit organizations made more sense, and cost less, than having the government create service positions. And finally, using federal dollars to pay for volunteers in existing non-governmental networks also encouraged private organizations, such as Habitat for Humanity, to step up their efforts with more traditional volunteers. In such a model, paid AmeriCorps workers could train and guide dozens of volunteers who, but for that guidance, might not be able to participate in a Habitat build.

I do not think that we have reached the upper limits of AmeriCorps, or future national and community service programs that are likely to take on new names, in terms of the numbers of people who would be willing to volunteer. We could expand the effectiveness of AmeriCorps with several simple steps. For example, as we saw with the Civilian Conservation Corps, to be effective, national service programs need to target pressing public needs. AmeriCorps does not always direct its volunteers to important national needs, and it could do a better job of tracking and publicizing the results it does achieve, and thus build greater public support for itself. What I found while I was at the White House and in the years since I left, was that using the names of actual programs, such as Teach for America and City Year, and highlighting pressing needs such as addressing the high school dropout challenge, were far more effective in convincing Members of Congress and the public to support these programs than using the brand name "AmeriCorps." The reason is that it is much easier to spot the needs Teach for America and City Year are addressing and the results they are achieving than it is to see what AmeriCorps is accomplishing.

More broadly, one of the lessons to be learned from the service programs tried in the United States over the past several decades is that there is power in numbers. Typically, many of the service programs we have do work independently of each other. That doesn't always have to be the case. AmeriCorps, Citizen Corps for homeland security, faith-based groups and volunteers in other programs and initiatives could be more effective than they are now if they join together around a common agenda and support the vision articulated by Freedom Corps. We need to increase support and provide more opportunities for federally-supported national and community service programs and for traditional volunteering.

Imagine if the proponents of various elements of the Freedom Corps – police chiefs, fire chiefs, emergency responders, Returned Peace Corps Volunteers, AmeriCorps alumni, Senior Corps advocates, mentoring groups, volunteers in national parks, veterans and more all joined forces to encourage government and non-governmental institutions to get behind a comprehensive service agenda linked to existing federal efforts to combat targeted problems. It would be a powerful alliance that could persuade Congress to truly embed community and national service efforts in programs across government. Voices for National Service, ably led by AnnMaura Connolly, does herculean work to fuel such a movement. Finally by 2009, a lot of this vision was fulfilled by the passage of the Edward M. Kennedy Serve America Act, which I discuss in more detail in the final chapter.

Ultimately, any program or idea depends on the response it elicits from citizens. Even though Presidential initiatives can be transformative for many, the most powerful citizen mobilization efforts often occur organically and in response to a great struggle or need. There are several grassroots citizen service movements that changed the culture and trajectory of America. One was the abolitionist movement. It spent decades working often on the political sidelines, but came into its own in the Civil War and the years after with its work to provide education and opportunities to freed slaves.

Other movements include those to put an end to abusive child-labor practices, give women the right to vote, extend civil rights protections to African-Americans, and, more recently, pass environmental protection laws. All of these movements had strong leadership, highlighted a great need, mobilized citizens in mass numbers, and worked to bring about change. And the results were stunning – the abolition of slavery, universal suffrage, the adoption of amendments to the U.S. Constitution, the passage of laws guaranteeing equal access to public facilities and schools, landmark legislation protecting the environment, and more.

This kind of citizen action in many cases had a far more profound effect on our country than the individual service initiatives of Presidents. But as William F. Buckley wrote in a conservative defense of national service efforts in an article that appeared in the New York Times on October 18, 1990, "The guiding purpose here is with the spiritual animation of the giver, not the alms he dispenses. The person who has given a year in behalf of someone or something else, is himself better for the experience."[lxxxvi]

Times of trial have always summoned the greatness of our people. War, disaster, economic depression, and other challenges have created a groundswell of neighbors helping neighbors and the environment for national leaders to call on the American people to serve their country. This was true during the Great Depression, World War II, and in the aftermath of natural and man-made disasters. It was also true for September 11, 2001, which would further awaken our civic spirits, making us, and our country, better for it.

8.

1933: Shenandoah National Park, VA. Franklin D. Roosevelt at a Civilian Conservation Corps camp.

9.

Oct. 14, 1960: Ann Arbor, MI. John F. Kennedy delivers a speech to 10,000 University of Michigan students, envisioning the future of the Peace Corps, at 2 a.m. on the steps of the Michigan Union.

10.

April 1964: Martin County, KY. President Lyndon Johnson's War on Poverty
began with a visit to impoverished areas where VISTA volunteers would serve.

11.

July 17, 1980: Detroit, MI. Ronald Reagan calls the spirit of volunteer service
a "deep and mighty river flowing through the history of our nation" at the Republican National Convention.

12.

October 21, 2009: Bush Presidential Library, College Station, TX. President George H.W. Bush and Mrs. Barbara Bush feature Points of Light with CEO Michelle Nunn.

13.

May 28, 2003: John F. Kennedy Library. President Clinton with a City Year team, an organization he helped support through the creation of AmeriCorps.

CHAPTER FIVE

Conscience and Culture

"[R]emember," President Bush told me one day in 2002 as we walked from the White House to the Eisenhower Executive Office Building across the street, "you are the conscience of the White House. You have to constantly remind people here, like people all across the country, that they have a responsibility to help their neighbors."

We were on our way to attend a service fair being held inside the White House complex that would both showcase different types of initiatives and encourage White House staff to set the example and get involved. But the President was making a general point. As the first occupant of the Oval Office to hold an MBA, I knew him as a leader who demanded measurable results. And to give him the results I knew he wanted from me, I would have to spend countless hours inside the West Wing winning support from overworked staffers who had dozens of other seemingly more pressing things to occupy them. Almost everyone was supportive of my efforts, but as the President was telling me, I would have to push my issues to the top of many to-do-lists.

Fortunately, I had a few key allies. To measure results, my colleague Ian Rowe tracked the progress of all 42 initiatives that were part of USA Freedom Corps and helped me compile quarterly reports on them. We could measure progress in programs funded by government, such as Senior Corps, AmeriCorps, Peace Corps and the new Citizen Corps for homeland security. My Deputy Ron Christie would keep tabs on progress with respect to appropriations in Congress affecting service programs. But to understand what was happening throughout most of America in terms of volunteer trends, we needed the Census Bureau (which is part of the Commerce Department) and the Bureau of Labor Statistics (which is part of the Labor Department) to include questions about volunteering in annual surveys.

The Commerce Secretary, Don Evans, was a childhood friend of the President whom I had gotten to know well during the 2000 presidential campaign. Back then he served as the campaign's chairman and had earned a reputation as a charming but straight-talking, tough leader. He was a brilliant businessman and loved America and its system of free enterprise. On one occasion, which fellow campaign staffer Dan Bartlett and I would repeat again and again, he summarized the campaign's strategy for a room full of staffers and then interjected something softer – "that George is just going to go around America and tell people what's on his heart." On another occasion after delivering a compelling but exceedingly technical briefing at the White House on the intricacies of trade policies aimed at preventing high-technology transfers to hostile nations, Don concluded by saying, "to sum up, basically what I'm trying to say is that anyone who loves America is a friend of mine." The room exploded with cheers and laughter. When I talked to him about what the Freedom Corps was trying to achieve, he quickly understood the importance of our work. He also knew that policymakers, business leaders and others would take our efforts more seriously if we had hard data, and that the President would insist on measurable results. So he agreed to work with the Census Bureau to ensure it collected the data we needed.

Labor Secretary Elaine Chao was also enthusiastic in her support. Before joining the administration, she had served as the director of the Peace Corps and headed up the United Way of America. Community service and self-sacrifice spoke to her personal story. She had come to the United States legally at the age of eight on a cargo ship, not speaking a word of English. Her father had left Taiwan earlier to seek better opportunities in the United States, and it took him three years before he was able to send for the rest of his family. One of her memories of the 37-day ocean voyage was seeing the Statue of Liberty come into view for the first time. With her support, the Bureau of Labor Statistics partnered with Census to establish the first annual volunteering survey for the nation.

In retrospect, the data that would be collected from 9-11 to the end of 2005 was very encouraging. But at the start of our efforts, we knew that collecting these data was fraught with political risk. With help from these Cabinet Secretaries, the Current Population Survey – more popularly known as the annual Census – would for the first time include an annual "volunteering" supplement. That supplement would measure how many Americans served through formal organizations (schools, places of worship and non-profits) each year, what volunteers did, what induced them to serve, and, for those who did not serve, what barriers prevented them from serving. With these surveys, we could compare levels of volunteering among states and cities all across America and foster healthy competition among them. We could compare levels of volunteering among age groups such as Millennials and Baby Boomers, the two large demographics in the country that had the best opportunity for moving the nation in a different direction and for helping to solve great national problems in the coming decades. We could measure rates of volunteering among individuals with different levels of education, comparing, for example, high school dropouts to those with four years of college. And, ultimately, we could evaluate the success (or failure) of one core component of Freedom Corps – getting more Americans to volunteer – and report it to the nation.

This was politically risky because the baseline for our measurements was September 2001, the very moment volunteering was likely to spike in the wake of the terrorist attacks. Many people expected the level of volunteering to fall off sharply by late 2002 and beyond as memories of the attacks faded. So we ran the risk of delivering volunteering numbers to the nation at the very time when there would be a strong, natural pressure for those numbers to fall. I worried that even as we advanced our 42 initiatives at Freedom Corps, the volunteering rates would fall. Robert Putnam, the pre-eminent scholar in these areas, fed my fears by warning of a coming fall in volunteer rates after the initial enthusiasm to serve in response to 9-11 waned. If such a drop occurred, we would be vulnerable to the criticism that our efforts were a flop. The data would be very useful, however, in giving the country a clear sense of where we stood and how we could adjust policies and practices to engage more Americans in civic life.

It was not necessarily politically wise, but it was the right thing to do, so we took the plunge, held our breath, and launched the survey. We were intrigued by the first batch of data – which came in December 2002. In the year that followed the terrorist attacks, the Bureau of Labor Statistics reported that 59.8 million Americans had regularly volunteered through a school, place of worship or non-profit organization.[lxxxvii] This number excluded anyone in national service programs such as the Peace Corps, AmeriCorps and the military. The data showed that most people volunteered because someone had asked them to do so. The biggest obstacles for volunteering reported were lack of time and the normal constraints people faced who had full-time jobs. At the same time, volunteering rates were also highest among those who were in the middle of their working careers and among youth still in school. Among organizations, faith-based institutions mobilized the most volunteers. My instinct, which had been to focus on mobilizing Americans where they spent much of their time – in schools, workplaces, and faith-based institutions -- had strong support in the first survey results.

Buried in the data was a fact that flipped a light on in my head. To be successful, I needed to win allies in the administration and win financial support from Congress. But if Freedom Corps was really going to help foster a culture of volunteering, we needed to figure out how to help people clear one of the biggest hurdles: not having time to volunteer. We needed to find a way for people to serve their communities inside their workplaces, schools, houses of worship, and other institutions, where they were spending a considerable amount of their time already.

Ray Chambers, a brilliant philanthropist who had been a leading force behind the Presidents' Volunteer Summit in Philadelphia in April 1997 and the creation of the Points of Light Foundation, hosted a meeting in his New York office to brainstorm on how to boost volunteering. A lot of good ideas came out of that meeting, including the need to launch an ad campaign and the value of creating an award for those who met the President's call to perform two years of service over a lifetime. But perhaps most importantly, we came up with several ideas on how to make institutional changes in workplaces, schools, faith-based organizations, and other places that would encourage volunteering.

Following that meeting, I arranged for the President to meet at the White House with several CEOs of large corporations. I presented our Freedom Corps' plan to the

CEOs and said that the President was not just interested in a public relations campaign, but in long-term, institutional changes in corporate policies that would develop a sustained commitment to service and civic engagement. We discussed how the framework of the USA Freedom Corps – scores of service programs housed under one roof – could be used to support corporate volunteer service efforts. Not long into the meeting, ideas were flying around the room.

One CEO suggested that corporations give employees paid leave to volunteer to boost educational outcomes in communities in which they worked across America. Others suggested that companies lead efforts to mobilize mass numbers of people and resources to target a particular need, such as renovating run-down buildings or mentoring at-risk children. Other ideas included highlighting how service programs are aligned with business interests, which would give companies an incentive to get more involved in civic affairs than they were. For example, fixing a failing school not only gives students a brighter future, it also provides employers with workers who will need less on-the-job training. Another idea was for boards of directors to adopt resolutions to change policies in ways that encouraged civic engagement across many divisions of a company. This would signal to all corporate officers that these new policies were a priority for the company, and thereby increase the likelihood that they would be long-lasting and taken seriously within the company.

Three major CEOs instantly saw the value of what we were trying to accomplish and realized it was different than volunteer service initiatives of the past. Bob Nardelli, CEO of The Home Depot, was one of them. His company had a strong service culture, evident in its support for employees who serve in the military and for others who volunteer for programs such as KaBoom playgrounds or Habitat for Humanity in their communities. Steve Case, the genius behind the creation of America Online, loved the institutional approach. He wanted to ensure corporate practices would change permanently and that the effort was self-sustaining. In his company, employees were given paid leave to perform community service and AOL senior officer, Ben Binswanger, volunteered to help convince other companies to join our efforts. Ken Thompson from Wachovia responded by giving 82,000 of his employees six days of paid leave annually to serve in their communities.

To help bring these corporate efforts together and enlist more companies to follow their lead, the President launched a program called "Business Strengthening America." As Teddy Roosevelt once pointed out, the President naturally has a bully pulpit. And Bush used it with this program to encourage companies to follow through on making institutional changes, encourage CEOs to take a personal role in making such changes, and ask each CEO to recruit two CEOs from other companies to get involved.

It worked. Robert Willumstead at Citibank, for example, responded to the call by having the usafreedomcorps.gov website address printed on 30 million ATM receipts. He also personally encouraged other financial companies to get involved in a Habitat for Humanity initiative that involved building homes in dozens of communities simultaneously. Mike Eskew at UPS focused on building new playgrounds for underprivileged children, cleaning up parks, and renovating rundown schools. An original group of 18 CEOs quickly turned into a movement of 800, and eventually more than 1,000. A bright young woman named Megan Campion ran the effort and held summits all across the country, at which I was tapped to speak. Companies that often competed with each other liked the idea of joining forces to strengthen communities and in the process created a quiet revolution that did not make a lot of headlines, but nonetheless helped a lot of Americans in new and creative ways.

To spark more service in our nation's schools, we reached out to former Senator and astronaut John Glenn to build on the outstanding work of his service-learning commission. We sent through the U.S. Department of Education the best research practices for how schools could engage their students in more effective service-learning – linking lessons and student reflections in the classroom with real world community projects on which they could make a difference. Married with new Presidential recognition – the President's Volunteer Service Award -- that students could earn for 50 to 100 hours of service in one year and then highlight on their college applications, Freedom Corps was working to institutionalize a culture of student service within our schools. We even tied these service efforts to initiatives to boost student knowledge of American history and understanding of how they could play a role in shaping it through their own service.

Steve Culbertson, CEO of Youth Service America, who had thought a lot about the role of service in schools and among young people more generally, made a compelling point and summarized our goals in a speech I heard him give in Washington in 2002. "We don't want to simply get kids to serve in their communities and keep dishing out soup to the same line of people," he said, "we want them to learn about the underlying conditions that brought them to that line in the first place and to get the kids engaged in solving the hunger problem." But ensuring that volunteer efforts are effective is harder than it might seem. Margaret Spellings, the President's close friend, at the time Domestic Policy Advisor, and later Secretary of Education, drove that point home to me with a biting comment. "Bridge," she said, "you can keep your kids who are picking up trash and doing all that sort of junk....I care about the teachers." It was crass but built upon Steve's point. We want Americans thinking about how they can solve problems, how they can innovate, how they can take on a challenge and bring their entrepreneurial instincts to addressing it. We did not want to just have people serving for the sake of volunteering.

White House Deputy Counsel Tim Flanigan made a similar point to me when we, and several senior White House officials, were volunteering to rebuild a playground in Washington, D.C. "Bridge," Tim said to me, "why don't we bring a backhoe in here for 30 minutes to clear the area instead of using 8 hours of senior White House staff time. Serving for service's sake isn't an effective use of anyone's time." He was right. In one respect, volunteering without regard to the results of the effort put in might make some people feel good. But if it isn't necessary, it won't inspire others to put time in on similar projects. What's more, it can be wasteful of precious resources that could be put to better use. To be effective, we needed to think strategically about how best to encourage service that can transform the lives of others and meet urgent needs.

And here, I knew we could learn from faith-based organizations. Faith-based institutions had been on the front lines of social justice since before the founding of our Republic. They were behind many of the key social movements that effected dramatic change – civil rights among them. Many of these faith-based efforts are effective on shoe-string budgets. Faith-based groups also understand the power of love and compassion and other attributes of human kindness that no government bureaucracy or program can instill. This is one reason why the President supported a controversial, but innovative faith-based initiative that worked to enlist religious organizations in government efforts to help the poor and needy. Working in concert with faith-based groups could help to meet the needs of the poor and suffering. Government could help to expand their capacities to reach more people in need. To do so, government would have to help level the playing field between religious groups and secular organizations in terms of how they could compete for government support and maintain their character as faith-based institutions. Taking this basic step could do a great deal to unleash the "armies of compassion."

To take that step, the President created an Office of Faith-Based and Community Initiatives in the White House, something the National Council of Scholars at Presidents Park in Williamsburg, Virginia would list, together with the USA Freedom Corps, No Child Left Behind and the AIDS initiative in Africa, as one of President Bush's most important legacies. The President also created faith-based offices in many departments and agencies and helped make more than $2 billion in federal aid available to religious groups. This money was not earmarked for any particular group. The President simply allowed religious organizations to compete for federal funds that were already set aside for social services. This was consistent with the Constitutional separation of church and state. Federal funds could not be used for sectarian worship or proselytizing. No faith-based institution could discriminate against any beneficiary because of their religious beliefs. For example, Christian non-profits receiving federal funds could not deny aid to someone because they were not Christian. In turn, faith-based institutions would not have to secularize their ranks in order to receive federal funds. Whether a non-profit religious institution receiving federal funds could hire only individuals who shared their religious beliefs and tenets became, and still is, a more complicated subject of debate.

John DiIulio, the first director of the faith-based office, helped bring religion back to the public square. He did that with several creative policies, including the creation of a

Compassion Capital Fund. That fund raised money to help non-profit institutions increase their ability to serve more people in need, such as mentoring children of prisoners. DiIulio also helped devise other key policies, such as giving a tax break to the tens of millions of Americans who donated money to charity but did not itemize their tax deductions. He also commissioned a report on how religious groups were evaluated when they applied for federal grants. Sunshine is often the best disinfectant, and in this case detailing how faith-based organizations were discriminated against in the federal grant process helped force a more level playing field. After DiIulio left the White House in 2002 (he had taken the job with the understanding he would not stay in the administration for long), Jim Towey took over as director of the Office of Faith-Based Initiatives. He built on much of the work that DiIulio had done, effectively drove the initiative forward, and held dozens of conferences and seminars around the country to instruct faith-based groups on how to navigate the federal grant process.

The legislative component of the faith-based effort stalled on Capitol Hill, however, and funding levels for many components of the initiative never reached promised levels. The faith-based armies of compassion were strengthened by the initiative, but as DiIulio first worried back in 1999 when the faith-based agenda was announced by Governor Bush in a "Duty of Hope" speech in Indianapolis, many of these armies remained "outgunned and outflanked." Mike Gerson, former chief speechwriter to the President and now a columnist for the Washington Post, summarized the fate of the faith-based initiative well in writing in his book, *Heroic Conservatism*, "the faith-based initiative was not tried and found wanting. It was tried and found difficult — then tried with less and less energy."[lxxxviii]

More should be done to support the faith-based initiative, such as real support for the Compassion Capital Fund that would increase the capacity of faith-based institutions to meet targeted needs. Signature service initiatives could be included in the State of the Union, providing money for them in the President's proposed budget, increasing the activity of the faith-based offices within departments and agencies, and connecting faith-based work more directly with a new focus on social innovation. Given Barack Obama's background, his party's traditional support for service programs, his ability to deliver powerful and inspiring calls to service, and the work he has done to advance the Serve America Act, the stage is set for him to become the service President.

To help spread the volunteer enlistment all across the country, we formed in 2003 the "President's Council on Service and Civic Participation," a council of outstanding Americans who were well positioned to reach millions of people through diverse channels. The council included Bob Dole and John Glenn, two men who epitomized service to country throughout their lives, Darrell Green, a Washington Redskins football star who had also started a foundation to help disadvantaged youth, and many other well-known Americans including Cal Ripken of the Baltimore Orioles,

Cokie Roberts of ABC and National Public Radio, Sean Astin from Lord of the Rings, Wendy Kopp of Teach for America, and Steve Young of the San Francisco 49ers. In concert with the Council's work, Peggy Conlin at the Ad Council provided what became a $30 million campaign that ran ads before movies, during baseball games, and on TV, radio and the internet featuring President Bush, Senators Dole and Glenn, New York Yankees pitcher Mariano Rivera, and TV star Angie Harmon. Some of the ads were powerful and inspiring. Others were humorous. But all of them asked Americans to sign up to serve through the USA Freedom Corps.

The President's Council received another boost when the President appointed Jean Case, President of The Case Foundation, to serve as its chairman in 2006. By the end of her term, more than 1.4 million Americans had received the new President's Volunteer Service Award for performing 50 or 100 hours of service in one year, and a new initiative, called "A Billion & Change" put America's corporate talent to work, providing *pro bono* time in strategic planning, accounting, computer technology and more to America's non-profits.

We also attempted to mobilize volunteers in areas of greatest need. There are 15 million children in the United States considered to be at risk of falling through the cracks and reaching adulthood without a good education or otherwise able to lead a fulfilling or self-sustaining life.[lxxxix] Research shows what common sense would predict – that a caring adult can make a big difference in the life of a child, socially, emotionally, and academically.[xc] I have seen examples of that all over the country.

One came at an event for Big Brothers Big Sisters of America. There a top police officer for Cincinnati stood before a crowd of 500 people for 30 minutes weeping as he told us about how his life was "saved" at an early age by a mentor who took an interest in him, became a father figure for him, and encouraged him to put his life on a healthy and productive path. In Columbus, Ohio, I met Mica, who at 9 years old had been unable to read until a mentor entered her life. The mentor came from Bath and Body Works of The Limited, which buses approximately 1,500 volunteers into Columbus each week to tutor children in public schools. When I met Mica, she was reading a year above grade level, showed exceptional poise and confidence for a child her age, and reported that she was teaching her mother and grandmother to read. Her teacher told me, "Without these individual mentors and tutors, many of these kids would end up like their parents – functionally illiterate and possibly in prison."

Armed with research, and inspired by the vision of John DiIulio, and with help from outstanding White House Fellows Stephen Poizner and Heather Graham, the President announced in 2003 that the USA Freedom Corps would spend $450 million over three years on an "initiative to bring mentors to more than a million disadvantaged junior high students and children of prisoners." The aim was to use the funds to help faith-based programs like Amachi, named after the Nigerian Ibo word that means "who knows but what God has brought us through this child," and school-based programs organized by Big Brothers Big Sisters, to reach children in need. Over those three years, approximately $250 million were provided for the school-based and children of prisoners mentoring initiatives. In a highly competitive fiscal environment, this was a significant investment. The initiative could eventually reach hundreds of thousands of additional children with caring adult mentors who could help transform their lives.

One review of 56 federal grant programs related to youth mentoring, including the two federal programs that received significant new funds under President Bush's direction, however has shown that the federal government needs to do more to achieve results. Many of the government's programs fail to track the numbers of disadvantaged children that are being matched with a mentor or to track the impact that this relationship has on student performance and other important outcomes in their lives. Our goal to reach 100,000 children of prisoners with a mentor was exceeded by November 2008, but our larger goal to mobilize one million new mentors was never met. We created a White House Task Force on Disadvantaged Youth that led to the passage of legislation, the creation of an office, and other action to bring the more than 300 programs focused on disadvantaged youth into a more coordinated effort to actually help the customer.

One of the largest obstacles to changing the culture is the view of "volunteer service" inside Washington. Often community service is viewed negatively or, at best, as an afterthought by D.C. elites. In policy circles, service initiatives are rarely taken seriously and nearly always scorned. This has been true for decades. To change that both inside Washington and across the country, we created and made available online a "Record of Service" to enable citizens to record their service experiences and count their number of service hours. On each page we put powerful quotes from leaders, such as Mohandas Gandhi, Martin Luther King, and Albert Einstein, as well as from Presidents who had talked about citizen service as being part of a virtuous and happy life. Our goal was to make service ennobling.

Many conservatives strongly opposed even voluntary, federally-supported service programs, which we saw with the strong GOP opposition to AmeriCorps in both the Clinton Administration and the early years of George W. Bush's presidency. In the Bush years, Steve Goldsmith and I spent many hours educating House members about the legitimacy and importance of service programs. Many members were not aware that programs that they liked, such as Habitat for Humanity and Teach for America, were also programs in which AmeriCorps members served vital roles. Most Republican members had good hearts and spoke eloquently about programs in their local districts. But they had not made the connection between those efforts and federal investments supporting them.

There were also thoughtful conservatives like Bill Buckley, who believed passionately that every citizen owes a "debt of gratitude" to the "patrimony." We met with Buckley and had a fruitful discussion about his persuasive book, *Gratitude*, and his policy ideas for increasing the number of people who volunteer their time and energy in service to their communities. He had been strongly supportive of national service in the 1980s and 1990s and advocated publicly for the creation of new national service programs.

USA Freedom Corps came about as close to a comprehensive service initiative as you could get without having mandatory national service and without triggering a rebellion in Congress. We made more than $1 billion in annual investments in federally-supported service programs, created the first comprehensive community-based platform for citizens to engage meaningfully in homeland security; created an online network to help Americans find local volunteer opportunities, and established a complimentary program to the Peace Corps called Volunteers for Prosperity, which by 2008 had grown to some 43,000 participants and is getting us closer to JFK's goal of having 100,000 volunteers each year work around the globe.

The result: USA Freedom Corps actually worked. The Citizen Corps, with its more than one million volunteers, is now in more than 2,400 communities nationwide and adopted by Governors in all 56 states and territories; Neighborhood Watch has doubled; the ranks of volunteers in police departments and fire departments are swelling in more than

2,000 and 1,000 communities, respectively; community emergency response team capacity has more than tripled, and a new Medical Reserve Corps is operating in more than 900 communities with more than 208,000 volunteers, making it one of the largest volunteer programs in the country, rivaling the number of volunteers in our national parks. The Citizen Corps was on the frontlines of disaster response in the aftermath of Katrina when other systems failed, with one local Citizen Corps in Harris County, Texas mobilizing more than 60,000 volunteers in 48 hours to care for the evacuees in the Houston Astrodome. Many observers would note that the volunteer systems were the backbone of the response at a time when the initial government response seemed to stumble.[xci]

Citizen Corps reminded me in some ways of Sargent Shriver's "Community Action" -- the locally-organized, anti-poverty program of the 1960s -- but was instead organized around homeland security. We had provided a platform and a set of ideas and some federal support to the Citizen Corps, but its success was largely dependent on how Americans in local communities reacted to it. Many Americans responded with enthusiasm and continue to make the system work. But for it to remain effective over the long haul, Congress needs to permanently authorize the program and then provide the small, but vital, funds it needs each year.

Senior Corps grew by about 40,000 volunteers to a total of 540,000, mobilizing senior volunteers to tutor disadvantaged youth and to help ill seniors remain in their homes and communities. This was not the 600,000 we envisioned, and putting aside our initial goals, it is tragic that our country is enlisting only a fraction of seniors in America, especially given the 78 million Baby Boomers who are starting to retire, are the healthiest, best-educated, mostly highly skilled generation in history, and have more time to give back. Harris Wofford, Robert Putnam and I, as representatives of the Greatest, Silent and Baby Boom Generations, respectively, issued a report in 2008 that found that the majority of experienced Americans (ages 44 to 79) believe they are leaving the world in worse condition than they inherited it and that tens of millions of them want to increase their volunteer service upon retirement. Citing the goals of USA Freedom Corps, we provide a 12-point plan of action at the community, state and national levels to engage older Americans more effectively.[xcii]

President George W. Bush enlisted Presidents George H.W. Bush and Bill Clinton to conduct a public campaign using USA Freedom Corps as the vehicle through which Americans could give aid to support people affected by the 2004 tsunami in Southeast Asia and to those hit by Hurricane Katrina in 2005. The American public's total, nongovernmental donations to tsunami and hurricane relief reached $5 billion.[xciii]

In the Rose Garden on September 17, 2002 (Constitution Day), the President also launched as part of Freedom Corps an "American History, Civics and Service Initiative," ably led by University of Chicago professor Amy Kass. This initiative was partly inspired by discussions I had with historian David McCullough and others, including Bruce Cole of the National Endowment for the Humanities, John Carlin and Susan Cooper at the National Archives, and James Billington of the Library of Congress. The idea was pretty straightforward. We sought to help young American history teachers become better acquainted with core ideas and heroes and heroines in U.S. history. To do that, we held summer seminars around the country and worked with the National Archives to make 100 "milestone" documents available to students and teachers. The earliest document was the Lee Resolution in the Second Continental Congress, which called for independence from Great Britain and led to the drafting of the Declaration of Independence, and the most recent document was the original Voting Rights Act passed in 1965. The National Archives also made lesson plans available to teachers who could easily weave them into an existing curriculum. The National Archives let the people vote on the most important documents in our history – the Declaration of Independence ranked first and the Social Security Act tenth.

As we worked, we found natural allies in and out of government. Senator Lamar Alexander, for example, had helped revive a tradition of freshmen Senators making a maiden speech on the Senate Floor with a major talk on the importance of teaching children American history. He took the lead in creating Presidential and Congressional Academies, which bring students to Washington to study history and earn college credit. U.S. Supreme Court Justice Anthony Kennedy and the American Bar Association developed "Dialogue on Freedom" to spark a national conversation of who we are as a people and what the American Experiment is all about. And Mortimer Caplin, a veteran who stormed the beaches at Normandy and who served as President Kennedy's IRS Commissioner, reached out to me. He is an icon at the University of Virginia Law School, having founded the school of public service there, and wanted to begin a discussion about how to inspire those in one of America's strongest professions to do more to serve others – lawyers. We also fielded calls from a wide range of business and academic leaders who were starting their own initiatives to support the USA Freedom Corps.

As the volunteering numbers for the second year after 9-11 rolled in, we collectively held our breath. And much to Bob Putnam's and my own delight, not only had the country sustained its levels of volunteering from the year after 9-11, the number of volunteers swelled by an additional 4 million Americans, from 59.8 million to 63.7 million from September 2002 to September 2003.[xciv] By 2005, the numbers were up to 65.4 million. This level of sustained increases in volunteering by young people prompted some social scientists to talk about the possibility of a "9-11 Generation,"[xcv] a generation that was adopting a culture of community service.

Volunteering in community and national service had grown significantly under President Bush's watch. By the end of 2005, volunteering in America was at its highest levels ever through the present day. These levels were high during the very period that President and Mrs. Bush, and iconic Americans tapped to serve on the President's Council, were asking Americans to serve again and again on TV, radio and in many public events. Freedom Corps was growing federally-supported opportunities for Americans to serve and connecting them to local volunteer service opportunities by zip code and areas of interest. I like to believe that Freedom Corps is one reason why levels of volunteering grew and were sustained after 9-11.

And more than the numbers, we were seeing a stronger America – disaster preparedness and response efforts ramped up; more mentors for disadvantaged children; businesses, schools and faith-based institutions chipping in to build homes and playgrounds and meet other local needs; Volunteers for Prosperity and Peace Corps volunteers tackling urgent issues like HIV/AIDS and malaria; and millions of Americans stepping forward to help in thousands of other ways that are difficult to measure at the macro level.

But there were difficult and even heart-wrenching disappointments. One of which was that by the end of 2005, the war was sucking all the oxygen out of debates about domestic issues generally and Freedom Corps more specifically. After a first term within the White House of active Presidential leadership, new initiatives, increased funding, and every sector working together to create a stronger culture of service, the calls to service suddenly stopped, new initiatives dried up, and not surprisingly volunteering in America declined precipitously during the second term of the Bush Presidency. It is difficult to pinpoint exactly why, but the fact that volunteer rates fell at the same time when the

White House focused its attention elsewhere suggests there is a strong relationship between leadership and sustained volunteering efforts. After volunteering climbed from an already high baseline of 59.7 million Americans (27.4% of the population) the year after 9-11 to 65.3 million Americans (28.8% of the population) by the end of 2005, levels and rates fell to 61.8 million volunteers (26.4% of the population) by the end of 2008. By 2010, the volunteer numbers were still flat-lining at 62.8 million volunteers (26.3 % of the population). The record after 9-11 is one of both triumph and tragedy, of extraordinary Presidential leadership and of a war that seems to have disabled further progress. Looking back, I am more convinced than ever that one essential ingredient to changing the culture is sustained Presidential leadership both within and across administrations.

Another disappointment came in the battle over AmeriCorps. It began for me at an inopportune time – while I was standing backstage waiting to deliver a speech at an award ceremony for the Points of Light Foundation. Rosie Mauk, the director of AmeriCorps, came over to me. "Bridge," she said, "I'm so sorry, but we overenrolled AmeriCorps by 20,000 participants and don't have money in the Education Trust to pay them." But before I could probe her for more details, I heard Bob Goodwin, the CEO of the Points of Light Foundation, on stage calling for me. My heart sank. I gave the speech, but largely just mouthed the words. I don't remember a single moment of that speech – I was thinking about the ticking time bomb that I now knew to be buried inside of AmeriCorps.

Later that evening I confirmed the truth with Les Lenkowsky, CEO of the Corporation for National and Community Service (CNCS) that oversees AmeriCorps. The program did not have the reserves it needed in a separate trust – as required by law – to pay the benefits that all of its participants would be due in the coming years. It was a little bit like a pension system not setting aside the funds it would need to pay retirees in the coming years. And it was a moral, fiscal, as well as political problem for us. The systems to monitor these fiscal arrangements had never been put in place and because historically there had been enough money in the trust to pay the education awards, no one in the prior administration had an incentive to create a check on the accounts.

Essentially, the issue was this: Congress required AmeriCorps to set aside funds it needed to pay benefits the moment a participant enrolled, rather than allowing AmeriCorps to pay the benefits due each year out of that year's budget. Under these rules, AmeriCorps was about $200 million short of the funds it needed. So the government had made a promise to some 20,000 volunteers that it did not have the means to honor. Some in Congress, the ones who wanted to let the program "die on the vine," seemed to be happy about AmeriCorps' predicament.

I wasn't for two reasons. The first is that the U.S. government had a moral obligation to live up to the promises it makes. And the second is that money talks. Even though Lenkowsky promised we could find a way to solve this problem, the possibility that we would have to halt enrollment in the program until Congress sorted out the fiscal mess meant we would send a loud signal to Americans that the government really was not serious about igniting more community and national service after all. Compounding that problem was the fact that the President was making it a priority to cement in place a cultural shift that appeared to be underway (and had even called for expanding AmeriCorps by 25,000). If we halted enrollment in the program or allowed it to wither for lack of funds, we would have failed to put many more Americans into productive service, undermined our own efforts, and given our critics many nails they wanted to drive into a coffin for what they wanted to become Ameri-"corpse".

For the year that followed, I probably spent upwards of 70 percent of some days working on the AmeriCorps problem. I had immediately alerted the President to the problem and had also informed Mitch Daniels, who was then director of the White Hous's Office of Management and Budget (OMB). Daniels had appointed the right folks inside OMB to look into the problem and I met with astute lawyers inside his shop as well as congressmen, congressional staffers, and those outside of government who understood the intricacies of the problem. These included RNC Chairman Marc Racicot, who was a tireless supporter, and Secretary of State Colin Powell, who had led an inspirational initiative called "America's Promise" aimed at helping at-risk kids.

There were a lot of outside allies. Alan Khazei and Michael Brown, co-founders of City Year, and their outstanding colleague AnnMaura Connolly, would help organize a broad-based "Save AmeriCorps" coalition that would eventually lead to Voices for National Service. Wendy Kopp ignited her Teach for America alumni to contact every key Member of Congress. The non-profits that supported and benefited from AmeriCorps funding got organized for the first time on a grand scale in response to this crisis. Without them, I could not have done the job I did internally to keep AmeriCorps a top White House priority, competing with funding requests for the war, anti-terrorism efforts, and dozens of other urgent issues.

In the White House, I irritated my colleagues, kept pushing for a solution, and simply would not give up. One day, David Hobbs, the President's chief legislative aide and a strategic thinker, told me, "Bridge, I wouldn't want to have to advocate against your position too often. You are relentless." Hobbs had literally 100 issues to push for in a tough environment and AmeriCorps was only one of them. I knew the President would want me to push hard to get Congress to support AmeriCorps, and I kept thinking about that day when we walked over to the Eisenhower Executive Office Building and he told me to be the "conscience of the White House."

The situation presented a classic issue for White House advisors, testing lines of professional loyalty and personal integrity. I was, after all, fighting for a program that was closely associated with former President Bill Clinton. We were also in an environment of war, the threat of terrorism remained high, and domestic programs across the board were getting squeezed out in a tough fiscal setting. Although legislation was passed in 2003 to save the program from very significant cuts, there was no appetite in Congress that year to provide funding for the over-enrollment, let alone meet the President's request to increase the program by 50 percent.

In the end, we got the money we needed, though not as quickly as we needed it. Late in 2003, after I met with key congressmen on numerous occasions, the President turned up the heat by making several calls himself to Capitol Hill. He also enlisted First Lady Laura Bush, who was a wonderful advocate for community and national service, to work the phones in support of the program. Their efforts paid off. They won promises for strong funding levels for the program in 2004 and even won support for expanding AmeriCorps to 75,000 participants, up from 50,000. It was a good result and we met the President's commitment. We recruited a smart, strategic manager, David Eisner, to come lead the Corporation for National and Community Service, which he ably did for many years.

Interestingly, AmeriCorps has only been increased to 85,000 positions, less than half the increase that we were able to get under President Bush, showing the pressures of this intense fiscal climate. These facts show how difficult a task it was to boost AmeriCorps to 75,000 and how much political capital it took from the President and First Lady.

The sharpest defeat probably came on a program we thought would boost our national security. As part of the Citizen Corps, we wanted to create "Operation TIPS" (the

Terrorist Information Prevention System) to enlist truckers, UPS drivers, postal workers and others regularly on public thoroughfares to spot and report information related to criminal or possible terrorist activity. Similar programs operate on a local level all over the country. Virginia has such a program that has helped cut crime along Interstate 81, a major trucking route. And D.C. snipers John Mohammed and Lee Malvo, who terrorized the Capitol region for weeks in October 2002, were nabbed near Hagerstown, Maryland, after police received two telephone tips from a trucker and an alert motorist. The problem is that a national TIPS program scares some people, who were rightfully concerned about their privacy. And when some of these people voiced their opposition to TIPS, our proposal fell flat in Congress. For us, we learned a valuable lesson. Any effort related to increasing security had to strike a proper balance between privacy and security. Nevertheless, I cannot help but smile to myself when I drive along Interstate 270 on my way out of Washington, D.C. Along that road you will see electronic signs advertising the state's TIPS program.

And finally, the arc the Peace Corps has taken over the past decade was deflating. We had managed to expand the program. By 2007, it was at its highest levels in 37 years, on a path of growth, and had re-entered East Timor, the first newly created country in the 21st century. It was also operating in many other countries, including those with significant Muslim populations, such as Morocco, Jordan, and Senegal.[xcvi] It had been strategically re-positioned to tackle urgent problems, such as HIV/AIDS and malaria. And it had entered into a remarkable agreement with Mexico to have an exchange of volunteers, instead of just sending Americans to Mexico. But levels of Peace Corps volunteers were not on track to grow to twice their number in five years as we had hoped and still remained very low at around 8,200. This, too, was unacceptable and disappointing, given the success of the program and the large numbers of Americans who want to serve abroad every year. The program was being well run by the smart, business-minded director, Gaddi Vasquez. It is always difficult and expensive to deploy people overseas. And it turns out that the program is just too expensive for many Members of Congress to get behind and support a sustained expansion.

One senior colleague in the White House called Freedom Corps "Bush's Volunteer Brigades." I wish it were true on two levels. First, I wish that we were up to brigades' strength everywhere in America – first responders, community ministries, mentors and tutors, and more. Second, I wish I could have done even more to help translate the President's best rhetoric and intentions into effective results that fulfill the promise of a civic reawakening. We accomplished some very important things, but we did not spark the kind of transformational change the country needs and we must learn from our nearly century-old experiments in community and national service and do better as a nation.

While my work at the White House was in good order, I realized that that was not true at home. I had been away from my wife, Maureen, and our three children, Caily, Fallon and Regis, for almost four years. In public settings, I had talked about the dangers of father absence, and yet I was an absent father myself. I loved my White House experience, felt loyal to the President and respected my colleagues there, but knew I would regret not having had the time with my children when they were growing up. I had been away while my oldest daughter had gone from childhood to a teenager and my other children had gone through some of the most precious years of their lives. I also realized that the creative expanding stage of Freedom Corps had run its course and that with the emergence of the war, domestic priorities would take a back seat. Everyone I know cites "family reasons" for leaving public service. And I think it is fair to say that just about everyone weighs how productive they can be in advancing a grand mission against the personal toll it takes on their family. At least, that was the case for me.

In late 2003, I told Andy Card I would be leaving at the beginning of 2004, and he gave me time at the beginning of a senior staff meeting the next day to let everyone know. After I spoke, Josh Bolten teared up a bit and gave me a hug, and Karl Rove did as well. Senior staff applauded so loudly that the President – whose office is a short distance away – called out to Andy to see what was "going on in there." It meant a great deal to me that my colleagues, with whom I had been through 9-11 and many trying days together, valued the contributions I had made to domestic policy and through Freedom Corps. Condi Rice and Steve Hadley, the President's national security team, came over to talk with me and said, "This makes no sense unless you come back."

Leaving was hard. I had grown to care for these people and to have an experience that must be akin to military service, in which you spend a number of years with people in a foxhole and are willing to do anything for them for the rest of your lives. Crisis bred closeness. These were friends for life.

I received a lovely handwritten note from the President after he received my resignation letter, which is a keepsake for my children and grandchildren, and he issued a very nice public statement upon my departure. I also had the opportunity to sit next to him at the Christmas dinner for senior staff in the White House private residence. We talked about many things, including the work of building a culture of service. It was a nice ending for my service in the White House.

In the thick of the 2008 Presidential election campaign, the candidates and some in the press criticized President Bush for missing an historic opportunity to unite people around the mission of service and sacrifice. They would say that he could have asked for more sacrifice, and instead told Americans to go shopping; and that he could have kept the spirit of bipartisanship and unity alive well beyond 9-11, but instead instigated a period of divisive and partisan politics. None of that is true.

The genesis of the "go shopping" myth was not President Bush, but TIME Magazine reporter Frank Pellegrini, who in the September 21, 2001 issue of TIME wrote a story called, "The Bush Speech: How to Rally a Nation." In the article, Pellegrini praised President Bush's speech to the Joint

Session of Congress as "the finest, strongest, clearest, several-times-chill-giving speech of his life." Pellegrini then goes on to share his perspective on each section of the speech. In the article, Pellegrini refers to the portion of President Bush's speech that talks about the economy. Here's what Bush actually said, "I ask for your continued participation and confidence in the American economy. Terrorists attacked a symbol of American prosperity. They did not touch its source. America is successful because of the hard work, and creativity, and enterprise of our people. These were the true strengths of our economy before September 11th, and they are our strengths today." Pellegrini summarizes Bush's phrase, "I ask for your continued participation and confidence in the American economy" into, "And for God's sake keep shopping." But that was not a fair summary and, what's more, Pellegrini was complimenting the President. He lauded Bush for telling the American people to uphold the values of America, to remain calm and resolute in the face of a continuing threat, and to maintain confidence in the American economy (which, by the way, is the engine that powers so much of nearly everything else we do).

In the context of a declining stock market, the loss of what would become a million jobs in 90 days, fears that transportation disruptions would paralyze the economy, and the fact that Osama bin Laden had said that the attacks had "shaken the throne of America and hit hard the American economy at its heart and its core," President Bush appropriately did urge the nation to remain confident and participate in our economy, but he never told the country to go shopping. Reporters repeated this myth again and again. I even called some of these reporters and shared the facts with them. Some stopped. But myths grow for mysterious reasons and, over time, this one grew to the extent that it obscured what the President actually said.

This was particularly unfair, given that George W. Bush after September 11 rallied the country again and again in an unprecedented number of speeches, events, and a multi-million dollar ad campaign that featured him and Mrs. Bush asking Americans to confront evil with great good and to serve causes greater than themselves. It was unfair based on the fact that volunteering in the U.S. grew significantly and opportunities to serve in existing and new programs supported by the federal government also increased dramatically under President Bush.

In his visit to Ground Zero, President Bush made a point to thank the thousands of volunteers for helping with the rescue and recovery effort. On September 18, 2001, he spoke in the Rose Garden to urge Americans to continue to volunteer and work to meet the nation's pressing needs by donating blood, giving to charity and much more. On September 20, 2001, he repeated his call for Americans to keep giving in his speech to a joint session of Congress. He created a clearinghouse for donations – libertyunites.org – and, as I discussed earlier, launched a program for Americans to help Afghan children. And by November he was dropping hints of his big announcement in the 2002 State of the Union Address, the creation of USA Freedom Corps.

For the rest of his term in office, Freedom Corps would become a signature issue for him. Over the two years that followed 9-11, far from "go shopping," President Bush led by example in dedicating a significant portion of his time and energy to creating, modifying, and publicizing service initiatives. [xcvii] I remember walking into the Oval Office at one point in 2002 to join the President and fly off on Marine One, the Presidential helicopter, and being stopped by Condi Rice. "Bridge," she said in disbelief, "another Freedom Corps event?" The "go shopping" myth was just that, a fable likely generated for political reasons in Washington.

And that fable has negative consequences that stretch past President Bush. He made community and national service a top priority of his administration, but by downgrading his work and his commitment, the mythologists in this case are diminishing the efforts of millions of Americans who heeded the call to serve and giving future leaders an incentive to not stake their presidential legacy to service initiatives. That is destructive because policies and leadership matter. Citizen service is important and every President has to consider the civic implications of his policies and continue the work that has already been done to make service a national priority. This is especially true in a time of war, when some sacrifices are needed from nearly all Americans. We have not done all that we could have done to connect ourselves to other nations through diplomacy, interfaith dialogue, and cultural exchanges. We have clearly not lived up to our potential as a civic-minded nation, but the places where we have made progress need to be recognized if we are going to make strides in the future.

History is writing the legacy of the USA Freedom Corps. Some social scientists are calling it the most comprehensive civic engagement initiative, measured by public investment and numbers of Americans mobilized to serve, since the CCC. Freedom Corps lived up to the test of the times. But the harder question is whether it will survive the ages. Both President Obama and Senator McCain promised to keep and expand the Freedom Corps on their campaigns. Thankfully, President Obama has, among other things, continued the Citizen Corps and its component programs, the Medical Reserve Corps, Volunteers in Police Service, Fire Corps, Community Emergency Response Teams, Neighborhood Watch, and Citizen Corps Councils. The Obama Administration continued the annual Volunteering Survey of the U.S. that we put in place after 9-11, and also signed legislation that authorized Volunteers for Prosperity, the international service program President Bush created by Executive Order in 2003, and supported the program in its budget. And the Obama White House has built on the new service office of the Freedom Corps by creating a White House Office of Social Innovation and Civic Participation and continuing the comprehensive clearinghouse, then called "volunteer.gov" under Bush and now called "serve.gov." It also continued the President's Volunteer Service Award and tapped Americans, of which I am one, to serve on the White House Council for Community Solutions to offer ideas. And the President has continued the faith-based office, a key component of the Freedom Corps.

The White House, however, has not used the extraordinary power of the new national service council that we created after 9-11 to develop and drive policy across government in part, I have been told, because many domestic issues are now the subject of individual offices and "czars." This is a mistake, because it will likely fracture support for specific programs when unified effort is what driving real change requires. The White House should use the new council's authority to effect change across government, including in promoting social innovation.

In the end, service depends on the transformation it can effect in a person. No nation can be moved solely through Presidential leadership or Congressional action. Progress depends on the choices individuals make to give back something to a country that protects our freedom and guarantees our rights. Finding that individual calling – uncovering your unique personal and professional path – is fundamental to sparking that spiritual animation and leading a happy life.

14.

May 30, 2002: Eisenhower Executive Office. Walking to a White House Service Fair, the President tells the author, "you are the conscience of the White House."

15.

March 12, 2002: Air Force One. Briefing the President on the way to a service-learning event in Philadelphia, PA.

16.

December 13, 2002: White House. The author awaits final comments from the President on proposed remarks.

17.

March 20, 2002: White House. The entire Freedom Corps team briefs the President.

18.

April 8, 2002: White House. The President, Ari Fleischer, Andy Card and the author walk out of the Oval Office to board Marine One.

19.

September 11, 2002: White House. First Year Anniversary of 9/11.

CHAPTER SIX
Finding Your Calling

Although working together is necessary both to solve social problems and to attain personal happiness, it is too rare in American politics today. In recent years, there has been a polarization that has led some on both sides of the spectrum to seek conflict over consensus and partisan gain over solution-oriented policies. This is fed not only by some people with strong ideologies in politics and on cable news, but also by a media frenzy that focuses on the theater of politics and thereby empowers the loudest actors on the stage.

Passion and ideology are fine, of course, and they have long been a part of our political process. They are even necessary in a democracy. But there is a point where dissension becomes a goal in and of itself and sound bites replace serious discussion of pressing issues for our country. And it is here where such dissension becomes destructive. Partisanship can hamper efforts to educate the public about important issues and stymie efforts to hold forthright, honest debates that will encourage Americans to find solutions to our toughest problems.

This leads to another phenomenon that we are now experiencing that gives me a lot of hope. People want to give something back to their community and country, but they wonder how they can make a difference. In a class at Georgetown University recently, I asked a group of 60 young people a series of questions. "How many of you want to serve your communities and country in some way – to give something back?" Almost every hand in the room went up quickly. I continued, "How many of you want to serve through non-profits, service organizations, schools…?" About three-quarters of the hands went up. Finally, I asked, "How many of you want to serve in government – either through elected or appointed office – in Congress, City Halls, in the White House or the Statehouse?" Only about five hands were raised. And even some of those were unenthusiastic or related to being appointed.

Here was a class of the new "9-11 generation" – a generation that was volunteering more, voting more, and showing early signs of being more civically engaged than the Baby Boomer generation -- and, yet, many of these students in a top university in Washington, D.C., had almost complete hostility for their government and the politics they were witnessing. When pressed, they explained why they were interested in serving outside of government. One student said, "I can make an immediate difference through Horton's Kids" (a local non-profit started by Karin Walser that provides mentors and tutors to disadvantaged children in Washington, D.C.). "Government is too partisan, too bureaucratic" and not that "interested in solving problems," another said.

I tried quoting my friend Cokie Roberts, who once pointed out that government service gives us the greatest chance to enact national and international policies that will have a positive influence on tens of millions of lives -- but I was still not able to break through. The students simply responded that national and international problems were "too big" for a dysfunctional government to solve and that they themselves were "too small" to make a difference through government.

So I tried a different approach. I told the students how I had navigated my way from law school to a desirable position in a New York law firm and then into public service.

In September 1987, I finished my studies at the University of Virginia School of Law and made my way to New York City. There I took a job with a law firm with the best of intentions of making a good living while also improving the world. I had been recruited by a sharp, committed lawyer named Jonathan Clarke, who had worked as a young lawyer on the Warren Commission investigating the assassination of President Kennedy. I assumed that movement between Davis Polk & Wardwell in New York City and public service in Washington, D.C. was common, not rare.

Everything in my Wall Street law firm was big – the number of lawyers in the firm, the amount of money for young associates, the mega deals between titans of industry on which we worked, and the reputations of the lawyers all around me. I was practicing law with some of the best legal minds in the world and working on transactions on different continents. While in the New York office, I was dispatched to New Zealand to help privatize the New Zealand Telephone Company; worked on a bond issue in Venezuela; and helped acquire a gold mine in Papua New Guinea. Before long, I found myself in Paris, France, where I worked for three years. There, I helped sell a diatomite mine in Iceland, worked with lawyers in Italy, Belgium, Germany, Spain, England, Japan, Hong Kong, and some far-flung places. I also did research for a case brought against the Soviet Union for the wrongful death of Raoul Wallenberg, a Swedish diplomat who had saved thousands of Hungarian Jews from the Holocaust by issuing them protective passports during World War II. He worked in Budapest and was arrested by the Soviets when they captured the city from the Nazis and died in 1947 under questionable circumstances. I even helped to save the life of a man from Africa, by arguing the legal case that enabled him to gain asylum in the West after his relatives were killed back in Ghana. We were able to prove he had a "well founded fear of persecution" if deported back to his home country.

Law practice does not get much more exciting than this, especially for a young lawyer. The benefits were rich. I lived in Paris, was driven around in fancy cars, made an excellent living, and was getting valuable professional experience while working with wildly talented colleagues and clients. And, fortunately, I was honing skills I would need in public service, including the ability to carefully define issues, marshal facts, make tough judgments, negotiate complex deals, write with clarity, and consider the public policy implications of decisions. I had no regrets for taking the path I did.

Yet, underneath all of this excitement and the crushingly busy hours was a feeling of emptiness. The work experience was all I expected it to be, but the work itself was not resonating with me. There were lawyers whose love of the law was a clear passion, like Gar Bason, one of the very sharpest Davis Polk partners. It wasn't my passion. I did not like negotiating deals, fighting with other lawyers, and rehashing the meaning of indemnities and legal opinions. But I didn't want out as much as I wanted in to something I truly loved.

For years, I had admired Ted Sorensen, President Kennedy's top aide and speechwriter. I wrote him a letter and asked for his advice. I said, "I want very much to serve our country in some way.... I find myself reading books on the Constitution and the Lincoln-Douglas debates, rather than Anatomy of a Merger and Securities Law Reporter. Do you have any thoughts about what someone with my background and experience might do to serve his country? I worry that much of my generation's talent is focused on the pursuit of the dollar." He wrote a beautiful response that began with, "Thank you for your thoughtful letter with which I sympathize" and ended with, "I hope very much that your desire to do public service will continue to burn brightly and be fulfilled in due time." One of his suggestions was to go work in Congress.

So I followed his advice and took what I told myself would be a one-year sabbatical from the law to become Chief of Staff and Counsel to an exceptional young congressman from my hometown of Cincinnati, Rob Portman. He gave me free reign to develop ideas, draft legislation, and build a talented team of people, including an amazingly smart and thoughtful legislative director, Jonathon Petuchowski; a veteran Ways & Means Committee staffer, Barbara Pate; gifted legislative aides Jan Oliver and Seth Webb; and two extraordinary aides – Melissa Bennett and Brian Besanceney – who would work with me in the White House and with another Portman senior advisor and friend, Deputy Chief of Staff to the President, Joe Hagin.

Portman was a strong leader and had many gifts – innately bright, easy going, knowledgeable about the legislative process; he had a rare ability to reach across the aisle and work with Democrats, even those who were actively investigating Republicans. After a 12-year stint in Congress, he would go on to be President Bush's U.S. Trade Representative and, later, Director of the Office of Management and Budget. Eventually, he would be the U.S. Senator from Ohio. He had found his passion in life. I stayed on with him in the House for five years, during which time I was able to get my feet wet in drafting new public policies through the legislative process.

As the 2000 presidential season heated up, I signed on with the Bush-Cheney campaign. The genesis of my transition occurred when I was asked by the campaign to help organize an event in Cincinnati on substance abuse prevention. Working with the Coalition for a Drug-Free Greater Cincinnati that I had helped start in 1995, we identified a local faith-based community center that had once been a corner where crack cocaine deals were made. I will never forget arriving at Lunken Airport in Cincinnati and seeing streams of local politicians lined up to greet Bush on his arrival. I quietly took a seat and waited for his plane to arrive. When it did, a campaign official came in the door and said, "Where is John Bridgeland? He is to ride with Governor Bush."

I remember meeting Bush for the first time – he was friendly, chewing on an unlit cigar and did not seem that interested in my policy briefing until I started talking about the role that faith-based groups played in transforming the lives of people who had become addicted to drugs. The topic clearly fired his interests, because he responded by firing a lot of good questions at me. Earlier that day he had just launched the first major policy speech of his campaign, called "Duty of Hope." He expressed his philosophy of governance when he delivered it: "In every instance where my administration sees a responsibility to help people, we will look first to faith-based organizations, charities, and community groups that have shown their ability to save and change lives. We will make a determined attack on need, by promoting the compassionate acts of others. We will rally the armies of compassion in our communities to fight a very different war against poverty and hopelessness, a daily battle waged house to house and heart by heart."

I moderated the event with Governor Bush in that small community center where the armies of compassion were assembled and demonstrated the power of their work to transform and save lives. I also sat with the future President in a room where the temperature hit about 100 degrees and the air was so hot that fans set up around the room did not make things much cooler. All that they did was blast us with hot air.

Over-all the event had gone well, but we were all sweating and I thought Bush might be a little agitated by the heat and ready to just get out of there. I certainly was and when the event ended I headed for the door and my car, only to be called back by Bush. "Hey, Bridgeland," he said, "travel with me son." We rode together in his van to a downtown fundraiser and he asked if I would consider working on his campaign. I had a family, a job I loved, and did not want to leave them to move to Austin, Texas. But I promised to visit the campaign. When I did, a few months later at the invitation of Josh Bolten and spurred on by Rob Portman, I was impressed that the top people there were extremely gifted and doing exactly what they were built to do. Josh Bolten had a brilliant policy mind; Karen Hughes was one of the most articulate communicators of ideas I had ever seen; Karl Rove had encyclopedic knowledge of every district and state in America and its political history; and Joe Allbaugh knew how to manage the operations of a campaign. Bush himself was a bottom-line man – he wanted to know what ideas we had to effect change and how we would measure results. I took the plunge and became Josh Bolten's deputy, helping to oversee the development of public policy on the campaign. I had a ball. My office was in a converted closet, but I loved developing new policy ideas and felt I had a knack for it.

Later, after the election, the President named me his Director of the White House Domestic Policy Council and, of course, a year later after 9-11 changed our priorities, as Director of USA Freedom Corps and Assistant to the President reporting directly to him. These positions gave me new opportunities to develop policy initiatives and work with some of the best minds in America. Two of the country's leading social scientists -- James Q. Wilson, my former thesis adviser at Harvard, and Robert Putnam, also of Harvard and the author of *Bowling Alone* – became key advisors and mentors. The work and the people were invigorating. Josh Bolten, who went to work in the White House as Deputy Chief of Staff for Policy after the election, had a quiet demeanor and an incisive mind. He used to relish looking up arcane words and editing people's sentences as they spoke. His wit, wisdom, and friendship made it a pleasure to serve as his deputy on the campaign and as his colleague in the West Wing.

On July 1, 2001, when I was on the Domestic Policy Council, I would note in my journal: "So far I have worked on Global climate change Cabinet-level review; faith-based legislation; the strategy on S.1 – No Child Left Behind; campaign finance reform; federal election reform; substance abuse policy and demand reduction and treatment; New Freedom Initiative for Americans with Disabilities; rules and executive orders in countless numbers; Everglades/National Parks; project labor agreements; immigration policy; Missouri River Basin; Veterans Task Force and 10 other issues." This was what I liked doing: generating policy initiatives, or refining and advancing existing policies for the President's consideration. I was drinking from public policy fire hoses and liking it.

What I wanted the students in Georgetown University to absorb was that discovering your passion is a fundamental need in life. How you awaken to it is a personal journey, but there are signposts along the way. You just have to find them. I think back to the activities in my life in which I lost track of time and place. I can think of moments in sports – tennis in particular – when I would play an effortless, perfect match. Or I can think of walks in the woods with my dad, looking for birds. Or I can think of playing, again and again, the speeches of John F. Kennedy and Martin Luther King, Jr., reading about political figures in history and longing to be like them or alongside of them, and wanting to make a difference in my school or my church.

In finding those things that I loved, I uncovered who I was supposed to be. When I was in the field of my bliss, as Joseph Campbell once explained it for me, magical things happened.[xcviii] Not only did I have confidence and become my better self, but all of these helping hands appeared – people emerging to help me in the journey.

I also discovered that we do not make our own lives. More often than not, if you are following your passion, good things find you. Shortly after the President announced the creation of Freedom Corps, I called Sargent Shriver and asked him to meet me at the White House. He entered the West Wing lobby with the air of a very distinguished man in a well-tailored suit. He had long before found his passion. After our meeting I wrote in my journal, "Lunch with Sargent Shriver today. Wonderful time! He is 87, but so vibrant. He told me the story of when John Kennedy asked him to come to run the Peace Corps. Sarge did not know what it would become. He had to create it. It was just like my job, and President Bush asked me in the same way. [Sarge] said his whole life has been that way....being asked – forced – to do things. Never had much choice. He said my life would be that way."

What I have come to realize and what I wanted the students at Georgetown to realize is that once you find your passion, you never work again, although you may expend more intellectual, emotional and physical energy than you ever did before. My work in the White House and leading Freedom Corps was time consuming, demanding, and exhilarating. It ignited my intellectual energies and gave me new life. I met Condi Rice at an event to help boost support for ending malaria deaths in Africa after I left the White House and asked her how she kept up her exhausting schedule. She told me, "I love what I do, I was built for this....it gives me energy." And that's our task – to find the life-enhancing work that makes a significant contribution to others and gives us energy, fulfillment and hope.

But, if you are to be successful, chasing your passions is not easy. What's required is hard, dedicated work stretching over a period of years and even decades. There is no substitute for hard work. My proudest moment while working in the House of Representatives was when an official from the Library of Congress remarked that our office checked out more books and other resources than any other office on Capitol Hill. He told us that the last time an office checked out as many materials as we did was when Theodore Sorensen was doing research for then Senator John F. Kennedy's office. Given Sorensen's letter to me, I found that to be a wonderful coincidence and affirmation that I was on the right path.

Breakthroughs always come after tremendous intellectual legwork (and occasionally quiet time to think carefully). We used these resources to learn everything we could about issues and to develop a robust legislative agenda. We wrote 9 bills that were signed into law, including the Unfunded Mandates Reform Act, the Drug-Free Communities Act, the Underground Railroad Network to Freedom Act, and the Tropical Forest Conservation Act. We reached across the aisle to work with Democrats, some of whom were shocked when they first received our call. One of my greatest pleasures was to work with Senator John Glenn, a Democrat from Ohio, and his extremely talented staff. Again and again, we found people with good ideas and intentions on both sides of the aisle.

After I left the White House, Tom Tierney, a dear friend, formerly CEO of Bain and Company, and then

Chairman of the Bridgespan Group, flew to Washington to give me a little advice. Three colleges had asked me to consider being their President; law firms, lobbying firms and trade associations were making attractive financial offers; universities were offering teaching posts; leading non-profits asked me to interview to be their CEOs; and part of me just wanted to stay home, play with my kids, read the newspaper and get to know my family again. After I had cleaned the basement three times and was ready to consider what I might do for the rest of my life, I adopted what we called the "Tierney Plan." It can be summed up in a few simple steps:

First, reflect on those experiences in your life when you have been totally engaged in something and have lost all track of time and place. Note them. See if there are any patterns.

Second, make a list of the people whom you have admired in life and what it was about them that you admired. They can be historic figures. What were their career choices and what did they achieve?

Third, do not take your journey alone. Reach out to mentors and friends, give them a context for your decision-making, and ask for ideas and advice. Ask people you may not even know but admire to meet with you. They often say yes.

Fourth, identify the key characteristics of professional employment – e.g., what I wrote out for myself was this: "want to lead, not just follow; can't stand bureaucracy; willing to take some risk; do not like being someone's deputy, but delighted to work with people of great talent; need platforms that enable me to create."

Fifth, make a list of specific opportunities, including ones that you design, and measure them against everything you have just noted about yourself. Remember the power of multiple platforms – you do not have to do just one thing.

Finally, find 20 minutes of quiet time each day. I find that in silence, transformations occur. Many people find this through prayer and meditation. I do both. However you find it – in a church or temple, in a park, or in your kitchen – take time to enjoy the peace and calm.

In my case, I discovered that what I wanted to do did not exist. I wanted to create a domestic policy council for the private sector – to do for non-profits, foundations, corporations and other governments what I had done for the President, develop innovative public policy initiatives that could make a difference in helping people. I did not want to lobby or work in a large bureaucracy. The mentors with whom I talked – James Q. Wilson, John DiIulio, Robert Putnam, Stephen Goldsmith, Harris Wofford, Amy Kass, Randy Teague, Bill Galston, and my father – all encouraged me to start what would become Civic Enterprises, and they offered to help. They knew I liked exploring ideas, developing new policies, trying to bring people from different perspectives and parties together behind initiatives that would help the country. Don Frazier, a good friend who had started his own business, helped me start my own and gave me the courage to do it. Follow your compass, they said, and we will help you.

In the first seven years, most of my career interests have found an outlet through Civic Enterprises, including interests I have had since childhood that I never thought would connect to my professional life. Through Civic Enterprises, I have been able to help low-income children gain access to quality and engaging education by publishing more than a dozen reports on the high school dropout epidemic, one of which ended up on the cover of TIME Magazine and on two Oprah Winfrey shows and led to a national movement, working with Colin and Alma Powell and Marguerite Kondracke of America's Promise and Robert Balfanz to increase high school graduation rates in the "dropout factories" where the problem is most severe. We have also turned our attention to working to increase the number of low-income Americans who complete college. We have partnered with the Bill & Melinda Gates Foundation, the AT&T Foundation and many others to move the agenda forward.

We have worked for the past seven years with the National Parks Conservation Association and its talented leadership on creating an initiative that gives both the private and public sectors incentives to preserve and restore these treasured landscapes and historic places -- what I call the collective consciousness of our nation.

Our company has also helped the AARP and others working to enable older Americans to have "encore" careers in national and community service.

We have surveyed veterans returning from Iraq and Afghanistan to figure out how well they are reintegrated into civilian life and what service they might want to continue to do on the home front to ease their transitions home and to inspire others. My former Chief of Staff, Mary Mcnaught Yonkman, who is a wife of a naval aviator, found her personal passion through this project and is now dedicating her life to engaging more veterans in service as they return home.

We have worked with the National Conference on Citizenship on the creation of a new Civic Health Index that measures indicators of civic life in America, such as volunteering, voting, charitable giving, social and institutional trust, and how well informed Americans are on critical issues. This has given me the opportunity to work with many bright Millennials, such as David Smith who with Maya Enista founded a non-profit called Mobilize.org. They are representative of a new generation of leaders who are developing their own non-profits to innovate and effect social change.

We also have been involved in a project that represents a childhood dream for me – the re-discovery of the once-thought-to-be-extinct Ivory-billed Woodpecker -- and are part of the recovery team working to protect it, working with John Fitzpatrick, Director of the Cornell Lab of Ornithology,

Hollywood film producer Bob Nixon, and world-renowned wildlife artist, John Ruthven.

I have the privilege of serving on 12 non-profit boards, with extraordinary people like Ethel Kennedy, Rick Warren, Tim Shriver, Harris Wofford, Cokie Roberts, Peter Chernin, Youssou N'Dour, and many others to do things such as working to end malaria deaths in Africa, working with disadvantaged youth in the toughest neighborhoods of Washington, D.C., to help clean up the Anacostia River, mobilizing young people for a year of national service to help other young people stay on track to graduate from high school and college, and encouraging more Americans to pursue careers in the federal government.

When you love what you do, you work harder than you ever have, and find that there is time for balance in life. You have a personal reawakening to the many possibilities in life and begin to pursue a happiness that connects you to others and makes you a force for the common good. You regularly feel you are just around the corner from a next great adventure.

What I also told those students at Georgetown and would later share with students at Ripon College in my commencement address, echoing themes I had shared with students at Saint Anselm College at their commencement in 2003, was that it is not enough to align your passion with your profession. Your life's work cannot and must not be only for the sake of your own comfort. In order for your life to have meaning, you must choose a life of service in some way. I have come across some remarkable people whose lives of service changed my life.

Consider Ray Chambers, a businessman on Wall Street who did one of the first leveraged buyouts of a company and was now wealthy, but completely unfulfilled. He dedicated the rest of his life to serving others. He mentored a young disadvantaged boy from Newark, New Jersey for 27 years from elementary school to beyond college graduation. He helped bring five former U.S. Presidents together to engage millions of Americans in volunteer service. When he realized how bad the malaria epidemic was, he got involved to save lives from the disease. He made all of these things happen through his will and leadership. Because of Ray's life, millions of lives on the planet will be saved. I asked the students at Georgetown and Ripon, "What is your life of service?"

I told them about another friend of mine, Bob Nixon, who was a Hollywood producer who made the film "Gorillas in the Mist." He came to Washington, D.C. and saw thousands of young people living in neighborhoods within view of the Capitol Building who woke up in the morning and went to bed at night to the sound of gunfire. He also saw that they lived on the banks of one of the most polluted rivers in America – the Anacostia. So he organized an effort that brought two endangered resources together – the young men and women who live in these violent neighborhoods with the polluted Anacostia River that could use their skills to clean it up. This Earth Conservation Corps of young leaders is cleaning up the river, educating others to help, and bringing the nation's symbol – the Bald Eagle – back to our nation's capital. In the process, these young people are discovering that even they -- children who were never told they were worth anything – could change their communities and save their own lives in the process. Thousands of young people who would not have made it beyond their neighborhoods are being given a second chance because of Bob Nixon. His is a life of service.

I also told students at Georgetown and Ripon that your life of service doesn't have to start when you're older. It can start now. My friend Wendy Kopp was in college and was concerned about the state of our public schools. She also believed that many in her generation would choose to be teachers in high need areas instead of more lucrative careers if given the chance to make a difference in the lives of children. So she wrote her senior thesis at Princeton about an initiative that would become "Teach for America." In the first year, Teach for America deployed 500 talented teachers in six low-income communities across the nation. Today, Teach for America engages more than 7,300 teachers and reaches nearly half a million students every year. Over its life, it has reached 3 million students. Good evidence shows that teachers from Teach for America outperform their counterparts in boosting student achievement. It also has built a pipeline of leaders committed to transforming American education, such as Michelle Rhee, who led the charge to reform our public schools in Washington, D.C., and David Levin and Mike Feinberg, co-founders of charter schools under the name of the KIPP Academy. These are lives of service.

My final thoughts for the students at Georgetown were that their instincts when they answered my initial questions were exactly right. America was founded on the belief that the individual citizen would address our most pressing social challenges. Americans would do what they do best – innovate, invent things, take action locally to improve their communities, serve others in need. I told them that government is not the place for innovation. Former House Speaker Newt Gingrich used to like to say that the Founders, who were concerned about tyranny, deliberately built a system of government so complicated, that no one person, party, or branch of government could make it work. Having worked in the Congress and the White House, I have seen firsthand that it takes extraordinary efforts to move ideas and issues along to successful completion. And those ideas largely come from innovative people and institutions on the outside of government, not from within.

Most productive change will occur in the small platoons of civil society, from the family up, not from government down. I shared with them that I had been encouraged to run for public office many times, but that putting aside the ego trip, I felt that my existing platforms through the non-profit and private sectors were far more effective at getting things done and enabled innovations to solve social problems much more than serving as a Member of Congress. So, I encouraged every student to find their passion, identify a great need, and perhaps even create their own platforms to effect change.

We need great people to serve at all levels – in local communities, in states and across our nation, not just in government, but more importantly in civil society that has been the bedrock of our democracy and public happiness since our founding as a nation. I told the students that while Presidents have issued calls to service, ultimately the desire to give needs to be internalized and become our call to service – our own reminders to use our talents to transform our world.

My sister has worked as a nurse with the sick and dying. She tells me that most of the people she sees on their deathbeds reflect on the love they have had with their family and friends, their connection to God, and how they had helped others. At the end of life, we want to know that we made a difference in life. Finding your calling will ensure that you can fulfill that human longing to make that difference. We know from neuroscience that such service is essential to human happiness. Such service can be mentoring a child in public schools. Or it can include signing up for a part-time or full-time position in a national service program such as Teach for America, City Year, Earth Conservation Corps or Habitat for Humanity. It can mean finding a job in public service, as a local prosecutor, a mayor or county commissioner or an official in state or federal government. It can mean serving in the military. Whatever it is, the path should ignite your own interests and passions because you will be good at what you do and you will feel connected to something beyond yourself.

After the discussion at Georgetown, many students lined up to ask questions about service initiatives. I took this as an indication that they were struggling to find their own passions but excited at the possibility of doing so. Some students probably did not absorb all of what we discussed, but I hoped they would at some point in their lives. Still others probably knew exactly what they thought they wanted to do and would have to discover for themselves, as I did, what their true path would be. I hope that what lingered with them from my talk was the thought of how they can best promote public happiness and unleash their own talents, and the talents of others, to address some of the toughest challenges we face. The health of our communities and country, and their own happiness as individuals, depend upon it.

20.

October 2007: Madagascar. Finding a new mission to help combat malaria, the author and Mark Grabowsky greet a mother and child coming in a health clinic for a bed net.

21.

June 2009. Rukara, Rwanda. The author and Dr. Steven Phillips, both board members of Malaria No More, distribute bicycles to community health workers and volunteers right after this ceremony to facilitate malaria control.

CHAPTER SEVEN

A Call to National Unity

Decades before becoming President and when he was still a registered Democrat, Ronald Reagan stepped to the podium to deliver the commencement address for the 1957 graduating class of Eureka College, his alma mater. He told the students, "Giving is a habit," and then exhorted them to "Get into the habit now." He explained that giving to important institutions in society was essential to the maintenance of our system of free government because those institutions serve as a conduit for passing our values and our liberties onto the next generation. "Democracy depends upon service voluntarily rendered, money voluntarily contributed," he said.

Barack Obama sounded a similar note during his first year in the White House, but with a twist. In talking about the destructiveness of dropping out of high school, he argued that it was incumbent upon all of us to become productive, well-educated adults because doing so helped society grapple with the difficult problems it inevitably faces. "[D]ropping out of high school," he said in his first major address to a joint session of Congress, "is no longer an option. It's not just quitting on yourself, it's quitting on your country – and this country needs and values the talents of every American."

Throughout our history our leaders, starting with George Washington and continuing more recently with FDR, JFK, Reagan, Clinton, both Bushes and Obama, have recognized the value and importance of citizen service. Many Presidents have launched service initiatives even though those initiatives have been routinely given short shrift by political pros, have seen their budgets slashed in time of war, and have not achieved the ambitious goals first envisioned for them.

The reason for the persistence of our Presidents is that active citizenship remains a cornerstone of our democracy and citizen service central to meeting national and community needs. What's more, in difficult times and during periods when there is sharp political discord, citizen service is one of the most effective ways to bind society together, make good on freedom's promise, and quell public anger or frustration. Mentoring a student in a failing school, for example, gives the mentor a window into the life of someone less fortunate than himself and also gives the student a better opportunity to earn a quality education, which in turn allows him to create a stake for himself in society by getting a good job, buying a house, and building a successful marriage. If done on a large scale, citizen service can promote national unity and purpose while giving more of us an outlet for our talents.

And there is another reason why Presidents perpetually put forward service initiatives. There have been periods of crisis in our history when they have been essential, and when large numbers of Americans stepped up to solve pressing national problems. As we've seen in an earlier chapter, one period was in the 1930s when FDR used the Civilian Conservation Corps to rebuild infrastructure and employ millions of young men during the Great Depression.

From all appearances, we are now reaching another period in American history when citizen service on a large scale will be essential for addressing national needs. With local, state, and federal budgets coming under increasing financial strain and the costs of health care, education, and other vital services rising, we may soon reach a point where our ability to address national problems will depend on our willingness to perform more citizen service. Volunteers, to give just one example, can help cut the cost of education by finding creative ways to bolster public schools. Voices for national service, therefore, need to be central to many of the debates we will hold in Congress, in state governments, and in local communities.

Civilian Counterpart to Military Service

One of the coming debates may be over compulsory citizen service. Across the globe, other countries are already creating a civilian draft for service programs. One of the most well-established is Germany's "Zivildienst." It dates back to 1961 and allows German men who object to the country's mandatory military service to apply for classification as a

Conscientious Objector. If granted, under this status they perform between 10 to 12 months of community service in Germany or abroad. Today, more than a third of eligible German men opt for Zivildienst, many of whom end up staffing the nation's hospitals and welfare institutions.[xcix]

In 2000, Taiwan became the first Asian country to offer an alternative to military conscription when it instituted a 5,000-member civilian corps for men with religious objections to the draft.[c] Guatemala passed a civil service law in 2003 that permits community service to be a substitute for mandatory military service.[ci] In Morocco, men who have completed high school can choose to perform two years of community service instead of 18 months of military duty.[cii]

Notice the trend. These compulsory civilian service programs are all alternatives to a military draft. Another idea I've seen debated involves creating a lottery system for citizens of a certain age who do not enter the military voluntarily. The citizens whose numbers were drawn would have to serve in a service program for a significant period of time – perhaps a year or longer. If instituted in the United States, this would maintain the military as an all volunteer force while creating a vast new civilian service workforce and force every young American, who would not know in advance whether their number would be selected, to think about what type of service they would like to perform. I favor this idea, because the debate alone might help prompt more Americans to voluntarily step forward and perform their year or more of service and create a culture of serving others.

But a civilian draft of any form would spark a heated debate in the United States as to whether it was warranted or even constitutional. Today there is no military draft and there is a deep consensus, across party lines, that favors keeping the military as an all-volunteer force. There is also case law that supports the government's ability to compel American citizens to fight in the nation's military, but not corresponding case law supporting a policy of compelling individuals to perform civilian service. So, at the very least, we could expect an extended court fight over any civilian draft.

What might be done, then, short of a civilian draft to encourage a more active and engaged citizenry? We know that people are more inclined to serve in response to some specific and great need, often born of tragedy and disaster. We know that the simple act of calling on someone to serve can entice him or her to serve. And we know that specific incentives – such as educational awards or money toward retirement – are relatively inexpensive to provide, but enticing enough to draw vast numbers of young people to serve their country.

We also know that it is extremely difficult to convince Americans to turn out for service initiatives if we do not first educate them on why such service is necessary and how it can bring personal fulfillment. Service has a way of connecting individuals to the larger story of American history that they can help shape. As President Obama has eloquently stated in describing his own service in communities, "And it wasn't easy, but eventually, over time, working with leaders from all across these communities, we began to make a difference -- in neighborhoods that had been devastated by steel plants that had closed down and jobs that had dried up. We began to see a real impact in people's lives. And I came to realize I wasn't just helping people, I was receiving something in return, because through service I found a community that embraced me, citizenship that was meaningful, the direction that I had been seeking. I discovered how my own improbable story fit into the larger story of America."[ciii]

But how can Americans, particularly young Americans, see how their service would fit into the larger landscape of American history if they do not know its story? One critical element of any service or civic engagement initiative must bolster efforts to teach civics and American history in our nation's schools and colleges. In April 2003, historian and friend David McCullough told a Senate Committee, "We are raising a generation of people who are historically illiterate." He went on to make the critical point we must all understand: "We can't function in a society if we don't know who we are and where we came from."

After 9-11, as I touched on earlier, we launched an American history, civics and service initiative from the White House that echoed through schools and communities throughout America. Going forward, we will need a much more robust effort from non-profit and private organizations and governments to instruct students in core American values, inspire them with stories of heroes from our history, and provide them the tools they need to participate in the life of their democracy, from local school boards to the Congress.

There are a lot of things we could do. A Presidential Commission could be set up that would investigate how effective current programs are at teaching American history and civics. The Commission could draw up proposals on how best to use national resources at our fingertips – at the Library of Congress, National Archives, Presidential Libraries and within our National Parks. State laws and common core standards could be changed to encourage and require civic and history education, provisions could be added to accountability standards to test the effectiveness of history and civic education programs, and adequate funding could be provided to ensure that such programs succeed.

But the goal must be to boost civic and historic literacy. One way to do that would be to take a hands-on approach. Schools could adopt policies that encourage or require 50 hours of both community service and civic problem solving each year (or 100 hours for older students), so that students can practice civic engagement. High schools would also have to work with admissions officers and college presidents to ensure that such commitments and Presidential awards for these service efforts are taken seriously. Community service work by students could become laboratories of civic innovation where, at a very young age, students see how they can transform their communities and country.

One innovative model of how students are integrating community service with classroom learning is found at the Cesar Chavez Public Charter High School for Public Policy in Washington, D.C., started by an immigrant, Irasema Salcido, who did not speak a word of English when she arrived in America at the age of 14 and now leads one of the best schools in the nation. Students from the school, realizing that the DC Public Library system was dysfunctional when they went to check out books for a school project and found the library branch closed, recently pushed for reform. They studied other library systems, petitioned and testified before the City Council with a series of policy changes, and saw their ideas become official policies of the D.C. government. The library system today is more functional than it was before.

The express purpose of Cesar Chavez is to give students the tools they need to make meaningful contributions to their communities. And from what I can see, the school is succeeding. When I met with students there in the aftermath of the DC Library service project, they were anxious to meet with other government and non-profit leaders because they knew from experiences that they could work effect change.

These models of service and civic engagement, tied to our history, could be expanded by the National Constitution Center in Philadelphia. The Constitution Center has fostered a partnership with a new charter school in Philadelphia called "Constitution High School," which focuses on civics and American studies. The National Constitution Center could plan an annual Constitutional Convention for students across the country. More such schools and initiatives tying back to first principles are needed.

How to create a culture of citizen service has long vexed many of our leaders, many of whom have turned to education as a means of fostering a civic-minded Republic. Today, a different form of a national university is being discussed and pushed by Chris Meyer Ash. His idea is to create a "U.S. Public Service Academy" built on the model of the U.S. Military Academy at West Point. Essentially, the government would pay the tuition of each student and design a curriculum around public service. Under this plan, the government would provide four years of education and a degree in exchange for graduating students agreeing to serve five years of public service in high-need public schools, low-income communities, disaster ravaged areas, or in government service. Such an academy would instantly attract top high-school students and quickly become a prestigious institution.

There is also no need to start from scratch. One way to get the academy up and running quickly would be to convert an existing university into the new service-oriented school or to create a consortium of many of the outstanding schools today that are trying to serve this same purpose – the Institute of Politics at Harvard's Kennedy School of Government, the Woodrow Wilson Center at Princeton, Schools of Public Service started by John Glenn in Ohio or Robert Dole in Kansas, among countless others. Along the same idea, Max Stier of the Partnership for Public Service and I have suggested that the government create a new grant program for graduate students called Roosevelt Scholars. The grant would cover one year of tuition for every two years the graduate student agreed to work in public service after finishing his or her studies.

There are other things, beyond public education, that we can do to encourage the creation of a culture of citizen service in the very places Americans find themselves every day and week. There are plenty of opportunities to expand service in workplaces and faith-based institutions.

Employers, for example, could make it well known that a person's service record is relevant to obtaining a job. After all, citizen service is not simply good for us individually and as a society, it is also a marker of a productive employee. Someone who has a track record of volunteering in his or her community is more likely to be a committed employee who is loyal and hard working than someone who doesn't have such a track record. Employers could provide ongoing service opportunities for employees, by supporting local volunteer efforts, or they could reward volunteer service with performance bonuses and company recognition. Corporations could also pick up on ideas that came out of early service debates in the Bush White House, such as adopting policies that offer paid administrative leave for community service, giving formal board recognition to new service-oriented policies, or encouraging company and board officers to serve on non-profit boards. The latter would do a lot of good, because it would likely build long-standing bonds between profitable companies and non-profit organizations. And companies could undergo an annual "civic audit," which would provide corporate officers with a detailed look at how civically engaged their company really is. The National Conference on Citizenship will provide an additional incentive for companies to institutionalize pro-service policies.

Companies now are often judged by where they fall on the list of Fortune 500. The National Conference on Citizenship will compile and release a list of the top companies that will make up the "Civic 100."

From faith-based institutions, we could see a shift in thinking and I believe the stakes are quite high. Too often today, faith-based groups place a high premium on financial contributions. But often volunteer time can be just as important and, more critically, effective at creating a culture of service. In practice, this would mean that churches and other faith-based groups would encourage their members to tithe their time along with their money.

In Rwanda, Rick Warren's PEACE Plan is finding this approach to be very effective in addressing pressing community needs like malaria. I visited Rwanda with Rick and later with his team to see firsthand how a country that had just emerged from genocide was transforming society from the ground up. One memory is particularly powerful to me. I spoke and then gave out awards to a group of faith-based volunteers who had been trained by pastors and community development volunteers in a little Pentecostal church in the Karongi District of Rwanda. When I came out of the church, the pastor pointed his finger up to a complex on a beautiful hill where Hutu militiamen without any intervention by the Pastor of the church had slaughtered thousands of Tutsis. A letter written from this location had inspired Philip Gourevitch's book, *We Wish to Inform You That Tomorrow We Will Be Killed with Our Families.*

Today Hutu and Tutsi volunteers are serving side-by-side to wipe out malaria. Their service is helping combat a disease, but because they were giving their time along with their meager funds, they were helping to heal their country's wounds by building personal bonds with each other. In Nigeria, prompted by Ed Scott's Center for Interfaith Action on Global Poverty, the Sultan of Sokoto, representing millions of Muslims, and the Archbishop of Abuja, with reach to millions of Christians, are partnering on an interfaith alliance to end Malaria. I thought about how these lessons could be brought to our own country.

The United States today is the most religiously diverse nation on Earth. But at the same time, our understanding of each other's religious traditions and beliefs is weak. Diana Eck has written on this topic and notes this fact in her engaging book, *A New Religious America,* and calls on us to "reclaim the deepest meaning of the very principles we cherish and create a truly pluralist American society." Her call is well founded. Religious diversity can either be a source of conflict, as we have seen time and time again, or one of the pillars of strength that can serve as an example to the world of how free people of different traditions and faiths can live peacefully together. To make our religious diversity a pillar of strength, we need to develop better inter-faith dialogue and promote volunteer service among people of different faiths to foster an understanding of the common principles that bring people to serve others.

Thankfully, some of that work is already being done. There are religious leaders and scholars who understand both their own faith's strengths and shortcomings and who are working to reach out to leaders of other faiths. Akbar Ahmed at American University, Rabbi Irving "Yitz" Greenberg of the Jewish Life Network, and Reverend Richard Cizik formerly of the National Association of Evangelicals are such leaders. Eboo Patel of the Interfaith Youth Core is also working to bring children of different faiths to work together side by side on service projects. His efforts and similar efforts across the country should be expanded.

Other bold ideas have emerged to ignite a stronger culture of service. Alan Khazei and Michael Brown, co-founders of the national service program City Year, have suggested creating something akin to the GI Bill, only this time as a reward for citizen service. They also suggest the government could create a pension system that would pay Americans a stipend upon retirement for public service performed over a lifetime (which harkens back to President Arthur's vision for the civil service). They have also suggested the creation of Baby Bonds, in which every child receives a bond at birth that they could redeem after they served their country in some way.

These would be powerful, albeit expensive, investments. But there are other ways we can encourage public service. One of which would be to expand existing programs. There were 215,000 requests for Peace Corps applications in 2002 and significant levels of interest beyond available positions continue to this day. The Brookings Institution, Building Bridges Coalition, Civic Enterprises and others have developed an agenda, launched on the 50th anniversary of the Peace Corps, that would ramp up the Peace Corps to 15,000 positions, Volunteers for Prosperity to 75,000, and mobilize 10,000 Global Service Fellows who would be tapped by Members of Congress, just like they nominate men and women for the military service academies. Together, these 100,000 Americans would help make volunteer service by people of all nations a common strategy in meeting pressing challenges in education, health, the environment, agriculture and more, and would lead to a more peaceful, secure and prosperous world.

We should enable the domestic Peace Corps, AmeriCorps, and new service corps to grow to at least 250,000 annually (as is contemplated by the recently passed Edward M. Kennedy Serve America Act) and eventually to one million national service participants. We should also better leverage the national service positions we already fund. For example, we could require that, where appropriate, non-profit organizations enlist 30 volunteers for every one AmeriCorps worker they employ with federal funds. This would be appropriate in the case of Habitat for Humanity where the objective is to enlist as many volunteers as possible to build as many homes as possible. The requirement would not be appropriate for Teach for America, where the objective is to enable qualified and inspiring teachers to teach in the toughest schools. If national service positions grew to 250,000 annually, such a leverage requirement could annually enlist more than 7 million Americans in service to the nation to tackle challenges that volunteers can help address.

The new Citizen Corps should be permanently authorized within the Department of Homeland Security and funded at up to $100 million a year for all of its components. It should be better integrated into emergency and disaster response training and the public "Ready" campaign. A cooperative agreement between Citizen Corps and the Corporation for National and Community Service would strengthen disaster response efforts. Citizen Corps is a gift to the nation and has showed its mettle in communities across America, including in the aftermath of Hurricane Katrina. Citizens responded to the President's Call to Service and his specific plan to engage them in homeland security. Now the government should do its part to support them.

The Senior Corps should be totally revamped. Designed in the 1960s and 1970s, it is not keeping up with modern demands. A first wave of 78 million Baby Boomers is already entering retirement.[civ] This generation of the best-educated, healthiest, most experienced and longest-living senior Americans in our history believes it is leaving the world in worse condition than they inherited it and could be enlisted to meet all sorts of challenges, perhaps most significantly by helping the 15 million disadvantaged children through mentoring and tutoring and helping millions of elderly Americans live independently in their homes as long as possible.[cv] Working with organizations such as Experience Corps, and the AARP, Senior Corps could create locally-based hubs of volunteer recruitment. Two-thirds of all older Americans and nearly three-fourths of those who are active volunteers use the Internet and nearly half lack information about volunteer opportunities. So there is an opportunity to use the information superhighway to plug these seniors into programs in their communities. Financial incentives, such as Silver Scholarships that they could earn and transfer to a child or grandchild, free rides on public transportation, and increasing the mileage deduction for charitable work to equal the deduction for business travel, would help grease the wheels of volunteer service by senior Americans.

In addition to the many investments in new and existing programs, Freedom Corps also created effective mechanisms to drive national policy and enlist successive Presidents to make community and national service a top national priority. The USA Freedom Corps Coordinating Council that President George W. Bush created, on par with the National Security Council, Domestic Policy Council, Economic Policy Council and Homeland Security Council, is unprecedented top billing for the national service community. This authority should be used to develop and drive new agendas. Presidents, too, should continually remind Americans that they have a duty to serve and sacrifice for their country, especially in a time of war. Administrations should also consider the civic effects of their policies and require "civic impact statements" for federal programs.

The National Constitution Center should become one of the central hubs for the online, citizen-centered volunteer service network that was started by the USA Freedom Corps at the White House and continues as President Obama's "serve.gov." This public asset enables every American to access one simple system and sign up for an array of federally-supported service programs. More importantly, since most Americans volunteer locally, they also can find local opportunities to serve sorted by zip code and areas of interest. Presidents eventually become unpopular in some quarters and having the online clearinghouse under the wing of the President may inhibit the participation of many Americans who do not share his values. Having a well respected outside institution be its home might increase its value. Presidents could still refer Americans to this valuable online resource, but it would no longer be viewed as the President's resource.

The National Conference on Citizenship, a non-profit created by Congress after World War II to keep the spirit of citizen engagement alive, has created "America's Civic Health Index." It provides an annual measurement of the civic health of our nation. We have regular indicators of economic health – job starts, unemployment, inflation, housing starts, and Gross Domestic Product. We should have regular indicators of civic health – volunteering, charitable contributions, trust in one another and in key institutions, membership in civic organizations, voting, civic knowledge, and more. These civic activities and attitudes help develop skills needed to make our democracy work, make market-based transactions less costly (by increasing trust among people), increase public health, and give citizens a common historical language from which to understand one another. These indicators build on the success of the Current Population Survey's data that has existed since September 2001.

The civic health assessment shows us that in areas where there has been focused national attention civic health can rise. Youth volunteering and political engagement have risen after 9-11, which have been targeted by presidential and congressional leadership since the devastating terrorists attacks, while many other indicators of our civic health have declined. What needs to come next is a dedicated, grassroots push to make solving specific problems a national priority.

High School Dropouts

One-fourth of public high school students and almost 40 percent of African American, Hispanic and Native American students fail to graduate from high school with their class.[cvi] Students at risk of dropping out need to be encouraged to stay in the educational mainstream. Quitting high school can quickly create the conditions that lead to a string of bad decisions that often lead to ill-health, drug or alcohol addiction, or even a life of crime. At the very least, it makes it harder for a young person to find gainful employment, and lead a fulfilling life.

Dropping out of high school takes a heavy toll on individuals, society, and the economy. College graduates earn on average $1 million more over a lifetime than do high school dropouts. If the students who dropped out of the Class of 2007 had graduated, the nation's economy would benefit from an additional $329 billion in income over the lifetimes of those students. The government would reap $45 billion in extra tax revenues and spend less on public health, crime, and welfare programs over the next several decades if the number of high school dropouts among 20-year olds in the U.S. today were cut in half.[cvii]

Sadly, dropouts are almost completely missing from the civic lives of their communities. People who quit high school vote less, volunteer less, and hold government office (either in the civil service or in elective or appointed office) far less often than those who get a high school diploma with their class. If dropouts are being failed by society – and they are – they are also failing to gain the skills necessary to work the levers of society to their benefit.

Fortunately, the dropout issue is now gaining far more attention than it used to. President Obama's administration is working to combat the high school dropout problem. A significant number of new non-profit organizations have sprung up around the country to push for education reform. And, after studying the problem, I and a few other individuals have found that there are a few key areas where a little effort could do a lot of good.

To start, John DiIulio, Karen Morison, and I studied the issue by taking a look at what motivates a student to quit high school. The result was a report, funded by the Bill & Melinda Gates Foundation, prompted by Marie Groark and Jacquie Lawling Ebert there, and conducted with Geoff Garin at Hart Research, titled *The Silent Epidemic*. That report concludes that most dropouts aren't giving up because the intellectual work is too hard. Quite to the contrary, many report being bored in class or seeing little connection between what they were learning and what they wanted to do with their lives. They wanted more expected of them, not less, and a more challenging and relevant curriculum. They also wanted their parents and other caring adults more involved in their schooling. Safety concerns and the lack of an orderly environment were also motivating factors for them. All of these are solvable problems.

We also learned in subsequent research that, contrary to conventional wisdom, parents with less education, lower incomes, and children trapped in low performing schools were the most likely to see a rigorous education, and their own involvement, as critical to their child's success. That leads me to believe that a focused and carefully thought-out approach, coupled with a strong demand for reform from local communities, could fundamentally improve our public schools across the country.

And we learned in our research that while teachers and principals understand the dropout problem in America and support many reforms, less than one-third of teachers believed schools should expect all students to meet high academic standards and graduate with the skills to do college level work. There is an "expectations gap" that is a significant barrier to closing the achievement gap. In our report, we outlined 10 policy reforms that could help more students graduate from high school ready for college and an increasingly competitive workplace. These and other reforms are going forward. It began with a National Summit on the Dropout Epidemic co-led by the National Governors Association, TIME Magazine, MTV, and Civic Enterprises, in partnership with the Bill and Melinda Gates Foundation, which sparked new action from governors, and new legislation and executive action from the Congress and U.S. Department of Education.

Thanks to the extraordinary efforts of Colin and Alma Powell and Marguerite Kondracke of the America's Promise Alliance, who are leading a national movement of 100 dropout summits in all 50 states, communities and schools all across America are waking up to the dropout challenge. Working with Robert Balfanz, Marguerite Kondracke, and former Governor Bob Wise, we developed a "Civic Marshall Plan" targeting what Balfanz had identified as the more than 1,600 "dropout factory high schools" and their feeder middle and elementary schools with the early warning and intervention systems, whole school reforms and infusion of volunteers and other human capital that can help ensure that we meet the President Obama's goal of graduating 90 percent of students in the Class of 2020 – students who are in the 4rd Grade today. The President is right. Dropping out of high school not only hurts the student who is quitting on himself, it is also damaging our country. It is time to act.[cviii]

Children of Prisoners and Other Disadvantaged Children

Over the past few decades, there has been a renewed push in this country to fight crime by imposing longer prison sentences, granting parole less often, and showing less tolerance for minor infractions than we had before. Judging by the results in New York City and elsewhere, many of the get-tough policies seem to have succeeded at reducing crime. But now it is time to take a second step in fighting crime by attacking an underlying problem that leads individuals to choose a life outside of the law in the first place. By intervening early and working with at-risk children, we can reduce the number of kids who grow up to be full-blown criminals.

And there is no better place to start than kids whose parents are serving hard time. There are as many as 2 million children in the United States today who have at least one parent in prison.[cix] The Bush administration took aim at these children with a program that recruited adult mentors. But that program has mobilized only 100,000 mentors. To succeed, the program needs to produce 20 times that number, which would give nearly every child with a parent in prison access to a mentor. This could be accomplished if the federal government fully funds its mentoring programs in the Department of Health and Human Services and the Department of Education and if large mentoring networks – such as Big Brothers Big Sisters -- partner with the government to recruit and train these caring adults.

There are 56 federal programs that have some connection to youth mentoring. To make better use of its resources, the federal government needs to examine each of these programs and report their success (or failure) in boosting academic performance, reducing crime, and increasing high school graduation and college entry rates. The government also needs to increase cooperation between federal agencies and develop a list of programs and policies that are effective. If the government does not do these things, enormous social and fiscal costs will come back to haunt us in larger prison populations, more illiteracy, higher dropout rates, less economic productivity, more welfare, and higher law enforcement and drug treatment costs. Volunteers need to be at the center of this compassionate initiative.

Global Health: Malaria

I have never seen a more powerful issue from a civic standpoint than malaria -- an issue where a single individual has volunteered to take it on in a manner than is truly mobilizing the world to end it. It is disease of sad contradiction – it kills people, yet it is fully preventable and treatable. Someone who is stricken with it might recover on his or her own or be felled for an extended period of time before wasting away. Worldwide, malaria kills one million people a year, mostly children under the age of five and pregnant women. Across the globe it infects upwards of 300 million people each year.[cx] But it is also a disease that is relatively easy to prevent and cheap to treat.

It has been successfully eliminated in many developed countries, such as the United States, and was the reason our own Centers for Disease Control and Prevention was initially created. As a result of the successful campaigns in this and other countries to eliminate the disease decades ago, today only 28% of Americans see malaria as a serious global disease.

By comparison, nearly 90% understand HIV/AIDS to be a serious threat to global health.

Malaria is an urgent health problem that can be solved with a focused and relatively affordable campaign. All it will take is an understanding of the disease, the will to act, some funding to support the interventions that work, and systems to monitor and sustain progress over time.

Malaria is a blood-borne disease. It comes from a bite of an infected mosquito. The mosquito's bite deposits eggs in the bloodstream of its victim, which hatch and kick start a process where the body works to fight off the invaders. The key to preventing the disease is avoiding the mosquito bite in the first place (Westerners who visit a malaria prone place for a short period of time often take antibiotics to ensure a bite never develops into full-blown malaria). And avoiding a bite can be as simple as sleeping under a bed net at night, when most of the mosquitoes are active, or spraying small doses of chemicals that kill the mosquitoes in places near where humans live.

Ray Chambers, a successful businessman and philanthropist with an ability to spot issues on which Americans can make a profound difference, launched a new non-profit called Malaria No More at the 2006 White House Summit on Malaria. He tapped me, along with my former White House colleague Gary Edson, to help engage the non-profit and private sectors in the summit and to build Malaria No More. Initially, Malaria No More worked to create grassroots support for malaria control, funding millions of dollars worth of bed nets. When Peter Chernin became our Chairman, Malaria No More was featured on American Idol, reaching millions of Americans with the opportunity to donate $10, buy a bed net and save a life, building on the successful work of a bed net campaign, run by Elizabeth McKee Gore and Kathy Bushkin Calvin at the UN Foundation, called "Nothing But Nets" that had been sparked by a powerfully written column by Rick Reilly in Sports Illustrated.

Malaria No More is also working in partnership with the American Red Cross, United Way of America, UNICEF, United Nations Foundation, the United Nations Special Envoy for Malaria and the African Leaders Malaria Alliance. The goals of the UN Secretary-General are our clear guideposts – provide a bed net to every African who needs one by the end of 2010 and end malaria deaths in Africa by the end of 2015. But it has not lost sight of the fact that individuals can make a big difference. In this fight, parents need to know how to properly install a bed net, what to do if their child has a malarial fever, and how to carry out mosquito eradication campaigns. Campaigns in Africa – Zinduka (A Tanzanian word for "wake up") and Night Watch – are helping to turn this disease of apathy into a disease that can be ended. Hundreds of millions of bed nets have now been provided to Africa, thanks in large part to the Global Fund, President's Malaria Initiative and the World Bank. Coverage of the population is not yet universal, but it is far more comprehensive than it would have been without Ray Chambers' efforts to spur the world to act.

And here in the United States, individuals can also make a difference. Nearly everyone can buy a bed net and donate it to the effort. Even children running a lemonade stand can raise money, raise awareness, or organize an effort that will help save an entire village in Africa. Bed nets last three to five years and they will need to be restocked. In addition to strong, continuing support from governments and other institutions, we need to create the 21st Century equivalent of the March of Dimes and demonstrate that the individual can make a difference in transforming the lives of children halfway across the globe. Tackling this large problem would boost our spirits and our national confidence. What I'd like to see is people wearing a sticker similar to ones we sport on Election Day. But rather than say "I voted today," these stickers would appear on passersby nearly every day of the year and read, "I saved a life today."

Service Nation

In September 2007, TIME's Editor Rick Stengel ran a groundbreaking cover story, "The Case for National Service," that provoked five presidential candidates to seek a briefing on service related issues from Bruce Reed, Tom Freedman (both talented domestic policy advisors in the Clinton Administration) and me. Afterward, I called Rick Stengel and asked if he would be interested in holding a summit aimed at drafting legislation and offering a plan on how to promote citizen service to whomever the two major parties nominated for President. He quickly agreed and then upped the ante. He guaranteed another cover story if the summit took place. It was extraordinary leadership from a top journalist.

At the same time, my wildly talented friend, Alan Khazei came to see me about his new enterprise, Be the Change, a non-profit inspired by Gandhi's call that "You must be the change you seek in the world." Alan wanted to build a new grassroots coalition and use it to push a bold service agenda through Congress and across the country. We agreed to partner and created what we called "Service Nation." The aim was to spark a movement of millions of Americans to support what Harris Wofford once called a "quantum leap in citizen service, cracking the atom of civic power."

Fortunately, we found key allies on Capitol Hill: Senators Edward Kennedy and Orrin Hatch, two well known and powerful leaders from opposite ends of the political spectrum. For months, we toiled away in back offices, worked the phones, and pulled in as many creative minds as we could to develop a series of policy proposals. We came up with several good ideas, including creating a fund to support a new generation of volunteers and building corps to work in health care, national parks, and public schools. We also hammered out ideas on promoting international service, an effort co-led by Lex Reiffel, Harris Wofford, and David Caprara at Brookings.

In the end, we came up with a 12-point plan that Senators Kennedy and Hatch introduced as the Serve America Act of 2008. One cornerstone of our proposal was to increase AmeriCorps to 250,000 people, up from 75,000. Among other things, the plan also provided funds to support volunteers working to reduce high-school dropout rates, created a stable source of money (the Volunteer Generation Fund) to underwrite service initiatives, and created a civic health assessment that would be compiled and supported by the federal government, in partnership with the National Conference on Citizenship. Taken as a whole, the proposals would create new avenues of service and give us yardsticks to both measure progress and highlight where we needed to do better. It was the legislation we had long sought to sustain the progress we had made in citizen service. It would engrain permanently in public policy the service initiatives rolled out over the past two decades, while also creating among millions of Americans the habit of service that Ronald Reagan and many other Presidents had urged.

Presidential candidates Barack Obama and John McCain quickly realized the power of the ideas behind what we had done and both appeared at a Presidential Forum on September 11, 2008 to show their support for the bill. TIME released its cover story at our Service Nation event, showing Obama and McCain in working clothes sharing "21 Ways to Fix Up America." TIME, AARP, Carnegie Corporation of New York and Target co-convened the effort, which was co-led by Alan Khazei of Be the Change, Michael Brown and AnnMaura Connolly of City Year, Michelle Nunn at Points of Light, and me at Civic Enterprises.

To push the bill through Congress, a coalition of more than 100 organizations, including the AARP, with its 40

million members 50 and older, got behind the service agenda.
Tim Shriver, Harris Wofford, Mike Gerson, Ted Sorensen,
and many talented young people helped craft a new
Declaration of Service in which millions of Americans made
their own service commitments and called on their
government, just like students before them did to help create
the Peace Corps, to provide more opportunities for them to
serve their country. Laura Bush, Hillary Clinton and Michelle
Obama all signed the petition.

ServiceNation gave us hope that America's finest
traditions -- what Rick Stengel called the "golden thread of our
democracy" -- can be preserved and extended to all
Americans. President Obama challenged Congress in his
February 2009 address to pass our bill. And finally, in March
2009, there was a flurry of activity. The House and Senate
passed various bills and in the end emerged with the bipartisan
Edward M. Kennedy Serve America Act, which Senator Hatch
had insisted on naming it. It fully reflected the work of
ServiceNation and President Obama signed it into law in April
2009 at an inner-city school in Washington, D.C., while
surrounded by the principal authors of the legislation, Senators
Kennedy and Hatch.

Senator Kennedy made two gestures that touched me
personally and demonstrated why he was such an effective
politician. As the Senate was voting on the bill, his office
invited me and other members of the coalition to an ornate
room just off of the Senate floor. After the final vote on the
bill, Senator Kennedy came in to meet us. I was standing with

my 10 year-old-son, Regis. Kennedy knew what to do right off. He greeted my son and when it was time to take a photograph of his senior staff to commemorate the passage of the bill, he placed my son into the frame. I have the picture still, Regis standing amid Kennedy's aides. Kennedy had even yelled, out, "Regis is part of the Kennedy staff." Senator Hatch was equally as gracious toward us. Although the bill was named for Kennedy, I and most other people in the room knew that Hatch had waged most of the floor fights to keep it on track – Kennedy had been too ill to do that himself.

Kennedy's second gesture came a week after the bill was signed into law. I was driving in rural Kentucky on my way to speak at a high school dropout summit when my cell phone rang. I wasn't going to answer the call. I didn't recognize the number, and besides I needed to focus on the event before me. But I picked it up anyway and was instantly greeted by a booming familiar voice.

"John," the voice said, "it's Ted Kennedy." He went on to say, "I wanted to thank you" for staying on this issue for a decade and for working on the bill. Three months earlier he had called to express his enthusiasm for the new national service proposal. Senator Kennedy then noted that we were "really blow torching this thing" called national service. He broke out in laughter. I got his reference to his brother, JFK, passing the torch of service to the next generation and laughed with him. The Senator's call served as an inspiration, so I told him that our group now privately called our efforts "Project Blow Torch." He loved it.

The bill that would bear Kennedy's name represented a quantum leap in the effort to engage millions of Americans in a culture of service. National service, after years of fits and starts, finally had its moment. It would take me 8 years, not the three I had in the White House, to help make this dream a reality. It was possible because of the efforts of many former Presidents who had made service and civic engagement a priority in their administrations. And it was achieved because of the many other leaders who devoted their energies to propelling the service movement forward, such as Sargent Shriver, Harris Wofford, Bill Moyers, Sam Nunn, Eli Segal, Gregg Petersmeyer, Steve Goldsmith, John DiIulio, Alan Khazei, Michael Brown, AnnMaura Connolly, Michelle Nunn, Shirley Sagawa, Bruce Reed, Rick Stengel, Mark Gearan, Vartan Gregorian, Tom Nelson, and Barb Quaintance.

Service World

President Kennedy said that his Peace Corps would be a serious enterprise when 100,000 Americans were serving abroad each year. With the Volunteers for Prosperity, we are getting close to that number. And it's an effort we need to continue. Service abroad is not only a morally worthwhile thing to do, it also serves our vital national interests in subtle but important ways. A large-scale survey of Returned Peace Corps Volunteers showed the Peace Corps has both a profound effect in fostering peace and understanding among Americans and people of other countries and has a transformational effect on those who serve in terms of their view of America, engagement in the world, career choices, and levels of volunteering over their lifetimes.

22.

September 17, 2002: Oval Office. The President and Senator Edward M. Kennedy moments before the launch of the American History, Civics and Service Initiative in the Rose Garden.

23.

March 26, 2009: U.S. Capitol. Many of the Service Nation team assembles in the President's Room off of the U.S. Senate Chamber after Senate passage of the Edward M. Kennedy Serve America Act, which would authorize many Freedom Corps initiatives. The author and his son, James Regis, are to the right of Senator Kennedy. Senator Harris Wofford is second from the right. Senator Orrin Hatch, fourth from left, led the Senate Floor debate, was the lead Republican sponsor, and recommended the bill be named after Senator Kennedy.

On 9-11, we were attacked by a group of terrorists who adhered to a tyrannical philosophy. Across the globe, hundreds of millions of Muslims live in fear each day of falling inside the grasp of that ideology. Whether it's a bombing attack in Pakistan, the rise of Taliban-like warlords, or the misrule of the Iranian regime, those who often bear the brunt of militant and radical Islamists are Muslims themselves. By volunteering abroad we give these Muslims and adherents of all faiths across the world a compelling reason to stand with us. Freedom is a precious gift that can bestow tremendous benefits on a people. As we spread it and the ideas that underpin it, we offer others around the world a reason to support free systems and free peoples. We gain a natural ally in our struggle to preserve our own freedoms by helping others preserve and enjoy the benefits of theirs.

Cross-border compassion will bring Americans and volunteers of different countries, cultures, races, ethnicities and religious beliefs together in common purposes. Such work will increase prosperity, lead to a more informed foreign policy and build a more peaceful and secure world. Our powerful coalition is now working to pass legislation that will boost international service efforts. The bill should be named the Sargent Shriver International Service Act to honor the man who, 50 years ago, built the Peace Corps.

The Gathering

Every year for the past five years, "social entrepreneurs" who have created new non-profits or other means to address urgent social needs gather to discuss their innovations and how to increase such efforts across the country. Organized by Vanessa Kirsch, the founder of New Profit, and supported by a coalition called America Forward, led by Kim Syman, these social entrepreneurs could unlock policy innovations that could improve education, health care, opportunities for the poor, conservation and stewardship of dwindling resources, and more. These extraordinary Americans – such as Bill Drayton of Ashoka, Wendy Kopp of Teach for America, the late Millard Fuller of Habitat for Humanity, Eric Schwarz of Citizen Schools, Alan Khazei and Michael Brown of City Year, Katherine Bradley of City Bridge, and Dorothy Stoneman of YouthBuild USA – have not waited for government to act. But government could learn a great deal from them. Americans have been inventing to improve their social conditions since settlers of the continent first reached our shores. Since the Mayflower Compact, individuals armed with new ideas have been at the forefront of improving our way of life.

Although an old tradition born from free enterprise, the spirit of social innovation now has Presidential attention and a White House office. And it's also off to a good start, notwithstanding some bumps in the road around grant-making and transparency. The Obama White House has created a $50 million investment in a Social Innovation Fund, which is very similar to the Compassion Capital Fund launched by the Bush administration in 2001. But government has to do far more to move from a status quo funder to a catalyst of social invention. It could be done in a few simple ways.

National service is one area where visible Presidential leadership is essential. President Obama has a tremendous power to rally people and inspire others to dedicate their time, resources, and energies in worthwhile causes. Presidents before him, especially President Bush after 9-11, reminded Americans of their duty to serve and provided more outlets for them to do so. The economic case for national service remains strong today. Hundreds of thousands of unemployed Americans could be put into productive work meeting national challenges at low cost to the taxpayer and through existing non-profits. National service has been shown to be a good bridge to full-time employment. Given the fiscal challenges we face and the need to get creative in meeting pressing public problems, national service provides a good answer to strengthen our civic health in hard times. And we can think anew about how such efforts could be scaled.

One of the most innovative approaches to spark reform that the Obama administration has tried is its "Race to the Top" program in education. This program sets aside a specific amount of funding, lays out definable policy goals, and then hands out the funding based on a competition among the states. This approach has a reach that far exceeds the amount of money at stake, because even states that do not win Race to the Top dollars implement reforms in an attempt to win the competition for those dollars. In addition to the current structure under the Serve America Act, the administration should take this same approach with national service -- setting aside funds for which states and non-profits could compete to generate the best results in addressing our toughest social problems. National service should become a means through which individual participants use their talents – and the non-profits in which they serve compete -- to innovate to solve social problems.

The President could create offices in departments across the government that examine how public policies promote (or inhibit) social innovation, and, perhaps most importantly, engage with Congress and insist that legislators consider the social innovation implications of the legislation they pass. A tax reform that incidentally wipes out an incentive for individuals to donate to a type of charity may be a worthwhile policy, but before determining whether it is, we need to know what impact it will have on existing charitable organizations and the ability of social entrepreneurs to start new charities. The annual Gathering of Social Innovators should be brought to Congress, so legislators can meet the extraordinary Americans from their districts and States who are transforming our communities and meeting public challenges. One social entrepreneur I know – Bill Drayton -- calls a charity or coalition that someone starts that person's "scratch on history." Every American should ask what their scratch on history will be.

A Final Word

After two tragic events at the dawn of this century – 9-11 and Hurricane Katrina – it became clear that the civic spirit of 1776 is once again vibrant in this country. There is no more caring, generous and charitable people than the

American people. And we have biology on our side as well to foster more cooperation and grow this civic spirit.

Americans carry with them an attractive optimism that has led us as a people to plunge headlong into vast challenges with full confidence that we will emerge successful in our endeavor. This optimism has long been demonstrated in war. Facing the prospect of defeat early in the Revolution, Washington assembled his men in the darkness and led them to make an icy crossing of the Delaware River, catch British forces unaware, and win a surprise victory that boosted national morale.

In the Civil War, running out of ammunition, Joshua Chamberlain ordered his men to fix bayonets in the Battle of Little Round Top that, according to historians, saved the Union Army and possibly the Union itself. In World War II, as Rick Atkinson writes in his book *An Army at Dawn*, American troops joined with the British to invade North Africa at a time when our military was akin to a boxer who had not been in the ring in a while and who had allowed himself to become flabby and slow. Yet, the Americans carried with them an optimism that Atkinson notes surprised the British and eventually aided the campaign's efforts to drive the Nazis off the continent.

But the optimism and can-do attitude have also long been on display elsewhere. In the 1960s, it was a shot that landed Neil Armstrong first on the moon that captivated the nation and the scientists and engineers who made it happen. It was a civil rights movement from the ground up, marching peacefully in the streets and attracting another peaceful assembly on our National Mall. Throughout the middle of the 20th century, Norman Borlaug, an American humanitarian, agronomist and Nobel laureate, did what once seemed impossible – spark a massive food revolution. The strides he made in farm productivity have likely prevented mass starvation even as the world's population has exploded over the past several decades. We have taken on enormous challenges as a country. The leaps forward we have made have occurred when bold goals were set and everyone pulled together. We must educate our young people that we can solve our toughest problems, and that we can work at all levels through non-governmental and government institutions alike to make a powerful difference in the lives of our people and in the Nation we love.

Service to others, rallying the armies of compassion, engaging citizens in the maintenance of the health of their Republic, and waking people up to care about the poor and needy are all fundamental to the health and vibrancy of our democracy and are the heart of our nation. They are also basic to our own human happiness and they connect our individual lives to the story of America.

We should get about the business of taking the next steps -- and be bold about them, keeping in mind George C. Marshall's charge to his State Department Policy Staff to "avoid trivia" as they proceeded to create the Marshall Plan that rebuilt much of Europe after World War II and helped unify the free world in confronting the Soviets during the Cold

War. We can again awaken the national consciousness to the plight of others and work across party lines to engage more Americans in service to our nation. Americans are longing for national unity and fulfillment in their lives. This sense of greater purpose is what our Founders promised, and hoped, when they exhorted the virtues of citizenship and penned the inalienable right to the pursuit of happiness.

Acknowledgments

This book would not have been possible without the help of family, friends and colleagues. First, my family – Maureen, Caily, Fallon and Regis – who lived with me through 9-11 and my White House years, which became formative experiences of their own. Also, to my father and mother, whose own lives of caring for others left a lifelong imprint on me. To my colleagues in the White House who supported these efforts, such as Josh Bolten, Gary Edson, Mitch Daniels, Condi Rice, Steve Hadley, Karl Rove, Karen Hughes, Margaret Spellings, Kristen Silverberg, and members of my Freedom Corps team, including Stephen Garrison, Ian Rowe, Ron Christie, Britt Grant, Lyndsey Kozberg, Katie Montgomery, Therese Lyons, Rhonda Taylor, Cornell Teague, Steve Poizner, Heather Graham and many others, and to my colleagues in departments and agencies who worked cooperatively to engage more Americans in service to their country, including Steve Goldsmith, Les Lenkowsky, Tom Ridge, Gaddi Vasquez, John Ashcroft, Elaine Chao, Colin Powell, Gail Norton, Joe Allbaugh, Mike Brown, Liz DiGregario, James Billington, John Carlin, Susan Cooper, and many others across government. Brendan Miniter served as editor, and Becky Schamore, Harris Wofford, and John DiIulio provided excellent suggestions to improve the book. Becky Schamore suggested the title. Keith MacLeod, a smart student at Harvard College who took my class at the Harvard Institute of Politics, volunteered to help me with the research for this book. Fred Brizzi, my assistant at Civic Enterprises, helped me with the final stages of this book.

Finally, I would like to thank the thousands of Americans I saw after 9-11 in communities across our country who were volunteering to make a difference and heal the nation.

Praise for Heart of the Nation

"John Bridgeland is a national civic asset and a model public servant. A talented senior official in the Bush White House, after 9-11 he reached across lines of party and ideology with the aim of transforming national tragedy into a new culture of service and citizenship. This book records his tireless and creative struggle, overcoming political cynicism and bureaucratic foot-dragging, to foster a new "Greatest Generation." He shows why that effort is important to personal happiness and to national renewal, and provides insightful suggestions for the way forward."

-- Robert D. Putnam, Harvard University, and author of *Bowling Alone: The Collapse and Revival of American Community* (2000) and *American Grace* (2010)

"As a gripping account of September 11, 2001, from inside the White House bunker and a powerful call to service for all Americans in the years to come, John Bridgeland's *Heart of the Nation* is a must-read for citizen activists, history buffs, and political junkies of every stripe. With wit and grace, he explains why the American people are so eager to give something back to their country, and outlines a compelling agenda to give a new generation of citizens the chance to do more. As one of the most successful social policy entrepreneurs in America and one of the most influential proponents of service in our time, John Bridgeland has shown us what a difference an individual can make – and his book is a rallying cry for citizens across the political spectrum to find happiness through common national purpose."

-- Bruce Reed, former Director, White House Domestic Policy Council, under President William J. Clinton

---

Heart of the Nation is an exciting and authentic account of a Presidential initiative to foster our civic spirit after 9-11 from a top official inside the White House. I know, because I was with its author nearly every step of the way. When the history of compassionate conservatism gets written, the efforts after

9-11 to foster a culture of service will be a vitally important chapter. As he did during his White House service in creating the USA Freedom Corps, Bridgeland connects national and community service to one of America's oldest and most important traditions – our desire to volunteer in local communities to help one another, and in that process, discover the means to our own happiness. The Founders thought citizen engagement was a bedrock of American democracy – and Bridgeland makes a compelling case for the re-ignition of the little platoons of civil society that can strengthen our communities and country. Read this book, absorb its lessons and your life will be enriched."

-- Stephen Goldsmith, former Mayor of Indianapolis, former Chair of the Corporation for National and Community Service, and Professor of Government at the John F. Kennedy of Government at Harvard University.

"Americans have always helped neighbors in need and rallied together during times of national crisis. But as the country confronts ever-greater domestic and global challenges, what can be done to make America's unique volunteer spirit and can-do civic traditions soar to new heights? How can average citizens, community leaders, philanthropists, corporate executives, government officials and others be motivated more strongly than ever to work together to achieve the common good both at home and abroad? Nobody in America today is better qualified to provide intellectually rigorous yet action-oriented answers to these and related questions than John Bridgeland. Bridgeland is a civic leader for all seasons who has won the respect of the many top leaders in both political parties who, for over a decade now, have consistently sought and benefited from his wise counsel. From creating local nonprofit organizations focused on revitalizing inner cities to founding the first-ever White House program dedicated to mobilizing volunteers all across the nation, Bridgeland has gained powerful and practical insights about what motivates good people to do good, how to forge inter-sector partnerships that make a lasting and positive difference in people's lives, and how to keep compassionate but cross-pressured political leaders in the fight to do what is right. Whether organizing leading researchers to develop better objective measures of civic health, or advising leading policymakers on how to solve specific problems like the high school dropout epidemic, Bridgeland has brought his front-line experiences to bear in ways that transcend polarized politics, bridge social divides, and get results. Now, in this meticulously researched and beautifully written book, Bridgeland shares what he has learned, from the streets of Cincinnati to the Oval Office, about what makes public-spirited citizens tick, and how government at all levels can do more to tap their energies and make real civic progress. Like its author, this critically important and fun-to-read book is brilliant, warm-hearted, and sincerely public spirited – a real national treasure."

-- John J. DiIulio, Jr., Frederic Fox Leadership Professor of Politics, Religion & Civil Society, University of Pennsylvania

---

"This lively story of John Bridgeland's life inside and outside the George W. Bush White House, shaping the President's call upon all Americans to volunteer for citizen service in response to the attack on 9-11-2001, is well worth reading. It's a powerful tale of a promising part of our history that connects the first President Bush's Thousand Points-of-Light initiative and President Clinton's AmeriCorps with the second President Bush's USA Freedom Corps that Bridgeland led, with the quantum leap in volunteering and national service authorized in the bipartisan Edward M. Kennedy Serve America Act of the first 100 days of the Obama Presidency. Bridgeland challenges readers to rediscover the idea of Public Happiness – the happiness that comes from participating actively in our self-government – which John Adams and Thomas Jefferson agreed they meant, above all, when they put Pursuit of Happiness, in capital letters, in the Declaration of Independence. Bridgeland brings that concept to life."

-- Harris Wofford, former U.S. Senator from Pennsylvania, Chair of America's Promise, CEO of the Corporation for National and Community Service, and Special Assistant to President John F. Kennedy.

Index

Q

R

Z

Notes

Chapter I

[1] The timing of these events were later described in the Report of the 9-11 Commission. *The 9/11 Commission Report: Final report of the National Commission on Terrorist Attacks upon the United States.* New York: Norton (2004).

[1] Langewiesche, William. *American Ground: Unbuilding the World Trade Center* (New York: North Point Press, 2002), 6

Chapter II

[iii] Langewiesche, William: *American Ground: Unbuilding the World Trade Center* (North Point Press, 1st ed., 2002) 7.

[iv] Kirkpatrick, Melanie, "*Sidewalks of Worship, Too,*" http://online.wsj.com/article/SB1000433220924889696.html>

[1] For background information on the Fund, see http://georgewbush-whitehouse.archives.gov/news/releases/2001/10/20011012-2.html.

[1] While more than 2,400 people were killed in the attacks on Pearl Harbor, nearly 3,000 died on 9-11.

[1] John Adams to Benjamin Rush, April 18, 1808, quoted in William J. Bennett, *Our Sacred Honor, Words of Advice from the Founders in Stories, Letters, Poems, and Speeches* (Nashville: Broadman and Holman, 1997), 25.

[1] Alexis de Tocqueville, Democracy in America, quoted in Jeffrey Brautigam, "Civic Education Initiative, Rebuilding Civil Society," Hanover College Center for Free Inquiry, <http://cfi.hanover.edu/civic/civiced.htm>.

[1] "William Henry Harrison," *The American Presidency, Grolier*, <http://ap.grolier.com/>.

[1] Robert D. Putnam, Bowling Alone: The Collapse and Revival of American Community (Simon and Shuster, 200).

[1] Robert D. Putnam, Bowling Alone: The Collapse and Revival of American Community (Simon and Schuster, 2000), see chapter 2, "Political Participation," and chapter 3, "Civic Participation," and also page 359; Robert D. Putnam, "Citizenship and the Six Spheres of Influence: An Agenda for Social Capitalists," Plenary Keynote Address, 2005 Post-Annual Conference Report, National Conference on Citizenship, <http://www.ncoc.net/>.

[1] Ibid.

[1] archives.cnn.com/2001/US/11/08/rec.bush.transcript/

Chapter III

[1] Library of Congress, *Hyperspectral Imaging by Library of Congress Reveals Change Made by Thomas Jefferson in Original Declaration of Independence Draft* (July 2, 2010) <http://www.loc.gov/today/pr/2010/10-161.html>

[1] Mortimer Adler, *We Hold These Truths: Understanding the Ideas and Ideals of the Constitution* (New York: Macmillan, 1987), 52.

[1] Mortimer Adler, Aristotle's Ethics: The Theory of Happiness-II, The Radical Academy, Resources in Ancient, Modern, and Contemporary Thought, http://www.radicalacademy.com/adleraristotleethics2.htm.

[1] Associate Justice Anthony M. Kennedy, "A Dialogue on Freedom," 2005 Post-Annual Conference Report, National Conference on Citizenship, http://www.ncoc.net/

[1] Thomas Jefferson, quoted by Merrill Patterson, University of Virginia, Interview with PBS, *Thomas Jefferson, A Film by Ken Burns*, <http://www.pbs.org/jefferson/>.

[1] Howard Mumford Jones, *The Pursuit of Happiness* (Cambridge, MA: Harvard, 1953), 21-26.

[1] James Madison, quoted in Jones, 26.

[1] Jones, 21-26.

[1] Quoted in Jones, 77.

[1] Quoted in Jones, 80.

[1] Quoted in Jones, 10.

[1] Quoted in John Hill, *Revolutionary Values for a New Millennium* (Lanham, MD: Lexington, 2000), 31.

[1] McCullough, "A Man Worth Knowing."

[1] Quoted in Jean Yarbrough, *American Virtues: Thomas Jefferson on the Character of a Free People* (Lawrence, Kan: University Press of Kansas, 1998), 3.

[1] Letter to Elbridge Gerry, May 13, 1797; Quoted in Hill, 68.

[1] Quoted in Hill, 88.

[1] Quoted in Hill, 69.

[1] Quoted in Hill, 91.

[1] Adam Smith, *The Theory of Moral Sentiments*, edited by E.G. West (Indianapolis: Liberty, 1976), 199.

[1] Smith, 204, 207.

[1] Smith, 313.

[1] Smith, 422-23.

[1] Benjamin Franklin, *Benjamin Franklin's Autobiography, An Authoritative Text, Backgrounds, and Criticism*, edited by J.A. Leo Lemay and P.M. Zall (New York: Norton, 1986), 72, 78.

[1] "Emory Brain Imaging Studies Reveal Biological Basis for Human Cooperation," Emory University Health Sciences Center, *ScienceDaily*, July 18, 2002, <http://www.sciencedaily.com/releases/2002/07/020718075131.htm>.

[1] James K. Rilling, David A. Gutman, Thorsten R. Zeh, Giuseppe Pagnoni, Gregory S. Berns, and Clinton D. Kilts, "A Neural Basis for Social Cooperation," Department of Psychiatry and Behavioral Sciences, Emory University, <http://72.14.209.104/search?q=cache:8uaOHqgLJJMJ:www.ccnl.emory.edu/greg/PD%2520Final.pdf+impulse+to+defect+and+achieve+immediate+gratification%5D&hl=en&gl=us&ct=clnk&cd=1&ie=UTF-8>.

[1] Sonja Lyubomirsky, Kennon Sheldon, and David Schkade, "Pursuing Happiness: The Architecture of Sustainable Change," *Review of General Psychology*, Vol. 9, 2005, 115-16.

[1] Lyubomirsky, Sheldon, and Schkade, 125.

[1] Christopher Peterson, Nansook Park, and Martin Seligman, "Orientations to Happiness and Life Satisfaction: The Full Life Versus the Empty Life," *Journal of Happiness Studies*, Spring 2005, 26-7.

[1] Christopher Peterson et al., 37.

[1] Martin Seligman, Tracy Steen, Nansook Park, and Christopher Peterson, "Positive Psychology Process," *American Psychologist*, July-August 2005, 416-19.

[1] Stephen G. Post, "Altruism, Happiness, and Health: It's Good to Be Good," *International Journal of Behavioral Medicine*, Vol. 12, 2005

[1] Richard Layard, *Happiness*, Penguin 2005.

Chapter IV

[1] Theodore Roosevelt, "The Man in the Arena: Citizenship in a Republic," Address delivered at the Sorbonne, Paris, April 23, 1910, Theodore Roosevelt Association, <http://www.theodoreroosevelt.org/research/speech%20arena.htm>.

[1] Ernst Ernst Fehr, Urs Fischbacher and Simon Gächter, "Strong Reciprocity, Human Cooperation, and the Enforcement of Social Norms," *Human Nature*, Vol. 13, 2002, 1-25; Samuel Bowles & Herbert Gintis, *A Cooperative Species: Human Reciprocity and its Evolution* (Princeton: Princeton University Press, 2011); Peter Hammerstein, Genetic and Cultural Evolution of Cooperation (Cambridge, Mass: MIT Press in cooperation with Dahlem University Press, 2003).

[1] George Washington, Farewell Address, 1796, Avalon Project, Yale Law School, <http://www.yale.edu/lawweb/avalon/jevifram.htm>.

[1] John Adams, Inaugural Address, 1797, Avalon Project, Yale Law School, <http://www.yale.edu/lawweb/avalon/jevifram.htm>.

[1] George Washington Will and Testament, "Rediscovering George Washington," PBS, <http://www.pbs.org/georgewashington/milestones/free_slaves_read2.html>; James Madison, Annual Message to Congress, 1815, American Presidency Project, University of California at Santa Barbara, <http://www.presidency.ucsb.edu/ws/index.php?pid=29502>.

[1] *Columbia Encyclopedia*, Sixth Edition, 2001-2005, <http://www.bartleby.com/65/ch/China.html>.

[1] Chester Alan Arthur, Annual Message to Congress, 1881, American Presidency Project, University of California at Santa Barbara, <http://www.presidency.ucsb.edu/ws/index.php?pid=29502>; Geoffrey A. Barta, "The Civil Service Examination in Song China," *AGORA*, Colorado State University, Issue 1, Fall 2001, <http://www.colostate.edu/Colleges/LibArts/agora/fall2001/barta.html>.

[1] (ch. 27, 22 Stat. 403), Cited in "Bipartisan Campaign Reform Act," *Harvard Journal on Legislation*, Harvard Law School, 2003, <www.law.harvard.edu/students/orgs/jol/vol40_1/comeau.pdf>.

[1] Theodore Roosevelt Association, http://www.theodoreroosevelt.org/research/speech%20arena.htm.

[1] Civilian Conservation Corps Alumni Association, "Roosevelt's Tree Army, A Brief History of the Civilian Conservation Corps," http://www.cccalumni.org.

[1] Franklin Roosevelt to Norman Thomas, 1940, quoted in Thomas H. Greer, *What Roosevelt Thought: The Social and Political Ideas of Franklin D. Roosevelt* (East Lansing: Michigan State, 2000), 18.

[1] Civilian Conservation Corps Alumni Association.

[1] "Founding Documents of the Peace Corps, Background," U.S. National Archives and Records Administration, http://www.archives.gov/education. Henry Reuss advocated for an active citizenry in a commencement address he would give at the University of Wisconsin at Milwaukee: "Pericles was right when he told the Athenians that the citizen who takes no part in public affairs is not merely unambitious but useless. If you will combine the private aim of getting ahead in life with the public pursuit of justice, you will help restore the essence of democracy – informed and lively participation by its citizens. And that can produce a government which feels compelled neither to do everything nor to do nothing."

[1] Remarks of Senator John F. Kennedy, University of Michigan, October 14, 1960, PeaceCorps Online, Independent News Forum for Returned Peace Corps Volunteers, http://PeaceCorpsOnline.org/messages/messages/2629/4078.html

[1] Peace Corps Timeline.

[1] "Founding Documents, Background," U.S. National Archives and Records Administration.

[1] President Kennedy's Remarks, Press Conference, March 1, 1961, PeaceCorps Online, Independent News Forum for Returned Peace Corps Volunteers, http://PeaceCorpsOnline.org/messages/messages/2629/4078.html).

[1] See "A Call to Peace: Perspectives of Volunteers on the Peace Corps at 50," Civic Enterprises Report, September 2011

[1] "Founding Documents, Background," U.S. National Archives and Records Administration.

[1] Harris Wofford, "The Politics of Service, How a Nation Got Behind AmeriCorps," *The Brookings Review*, Fall 2002, Vol. 20, No. 4.

[1] Peace Corps Timeline, Peace Corps Official History, www.peacecorps.gov.

[1] "Hoover Declines Peace Corps Post," *The New York***Error! Bookmark not defined.** *Times*, March 11, 1961.

[1] Peace Corps Timeline; U.S. Department of State, Bureau of Intelligence and Research, "Independent States in the World," <http://geography.about.com/gi/dynamic/offsite.htm?zi=1/XJ&sdn=geography&zu=ht tp%3A%2F%2Fwww.state.gov%2Fs%2Finr%2Frls%2F4250.htm.> 193 is the number of independent states in the world recognized by the U.S. State Department.

[1] Peace Corps Timeline.

[1] Hedrick Smith, "New Peace Corps Faces Opposition," *The New York Times*, December 26, 1962.

[1] Hedrick Smith, "Domestic Peace Corps Program, Slow in Starting, is Meeting Obstacles of Opposition and Confusion," *The New York***Error! Bookmark not defined.** *Times*, March 22, 1963; "Support for Peace Corps," *The New York Times*, November 27, 1962.

[1] War on Poverty: From the Great Society to the Great Recession. Transcript. American RadioWorks, http://americanradioworks.publicradio.org/features/poverty/transcript.html

[1] Marjorie Hunter, "Drive on Poverty Gets Volunteers, More Than 300 Offer Aid in Domestic Service Plan," *The New York*Error! Bookmark not defined. *Times*, August 17, 1964.

[1] Charles Mohr, "President Spurs Poverty Fighters; He Defines Tasks for VISTA and Opportunity Groups," *The New York*Error! Bookmark not defined. *Times*, December 13, 1964.

[1] Johnson quoted in *The New York*Error! Bookmark not defined. *Times*, December 13, 1964.

[1] AmeriCorps Programs, http://www.americorps.gov/about/programs/vista.asp.

[1] Senior Corps Official History Index, http://www.seniorcorps.org/about/sc/index.asp.

[1] See John M. Bridgeland, Robert D. Putnam, Harris L. Wofford, *More to Give: Tapping the Talents of the Baby Boomer, Silent and Greatest Generation*. Civic Enterprises in association with Peter D. Hart Research Associates. September 2008.

[1] George H.W. Bush, Acceptance Speech, August 18, 1988, quoted in *The New York Times*, December 8, 1992.

[1] "976 Points of Light-And Counting," *The New York*Error! Bookmark not defined. *Times*, December 8, 1992.

[1] "Investing in Idealism," *The New York*Error! Bookmark not defined. *Times*, November 30, 1990; Helen Dewar, "Senate Debates Programs to Promote Volunteerism," *The Washington Post*, February 27, 1990.

[1] National and Community Service Trust Act, THOMAS Legislative History, http://thomas.loc.gov/.

[1] President Clinton's Remarks, New Orleans, April 30, 1993, quoted in Thomas Friedman, "Also Urges Lending; $10,000 Grants Planned in Return for 2 Years in Community Jobs Clinton Offers New Plan to Aid College Students," *The New York*Error! Bookmark not defined. *Times*, May 1, 1993.

[1] Friedman, "Also Urges Lending," *The New York*Error! Bookmark not defined. *Times*, May 1, 1993; Michael Wines, "Clinton Honors First Members of National Service Program," *The New York Times*, September 12, 1994.

[1] Newt Gingrich quoted in *Newsweek*, as reported by Douglas Jehl, "Clinton Says Budget Cutters Should Spare Service Plan," *The New York Times*, January 17, 1995.

[1] William F. Buckley, Jr., "National Debt, National Service," editorial, *The New York Times*, October 18, 1990.

Chapter V

[1] Bureau of Labor Statistics, U.S. Department of Labor, 2002, quoted in "New Benchmark in Volunteer Service," Corporation for National and Community Service, December 18, 2002, <http://www.nationalservice.gov/about/newsroom/releases_detail.asp?tbl_pr_id=118>.

[1] Michael J. Gerson, Heroic Conservatism: Why Republicans Need to Embrace America's Ideals (And Why They Deserve to Fail If They Don't). Harper Collins, 2008.

[1] President George W. Bush, "Rallying the Armies of Compassion," The White House, <http://www.whitehouse.gov/news/reports/faithbased.html>.

[1] MENTOR, "How To Close America's Mentoring Gap," National Agenda, <www.mentoring.org/leaders/files/nationalagenda.pdf>.

[1] See "The Role of the Harris County Citizen Corps (pp.7-9) in Statement of Robert A. Eckels, County Judge, Harris County, TX before the U.S. House of Representatives Committee on Homeland Security: Hearing on Federalism and Disaster Response: Examining the Roles and Responsibilities of Local, State, and Federal Agencies. October 19, 2005.

[1] See Bridgeland, J., R. Putnam and H. Wofford, *More to Give: Tapping the Talents of the Baby Boomer, Silent and Greatest Generations.* Commissioned by the AARP. 2008.

[1] "Sweet Charity," *The Wall Street Journal*, December 24, 2005, <http://www.opinionjournal.com/weekend/hottopic/?id=110007728>.

[1] Bureau of Labor Statistics, U.S. Department of Labor, quoted in Robert D. Putnam and John M. Bridgeland, "A Nation of Doers Needs to Do More," *The Philadelphia Inquirer*, December 3, 2004, <http://www.ksg.harvard.edu/news/opeds/2004/putnam_inquirer_120304.htm>.

[1] USA Freedom Corps, "New Federal Report Outlines Economic Benefit of Volunteering in America," June 12, 2006, <http://www.usafreedomcorps.gov/about_usafc/newsroom/announcements_dynamic.asp?ID=1351>.

[1] "Predominantly Muslim Countries," Paul D. Coverdell World Wise Schools, Peace Corps, <http://www.peacecorps.gov/wws/lessons/learn_about_islam.html>.

[1] Just to highlight a few, in addition to his 2002 State of the Union Address, January 30 events in Winston-Salem, North Carolina to 20,00 people asking them to serve, a meeting with a Citizen Corps roundtable, and in Daytona Beach, Florida, later that day asking seniors to get involved in Freedom Corps; a January 31 event at Booker T. Washington High School highlighting the power of volunteering; a March 12 event in Philadelphia highlighting service-learning and volunteering; an April 9 event in Bridgeport, Connecticut discussing how service and volunteering are integral to the American character; June 1 weekly radio address discussing the culture of service; June 14 commencement address at Ohio State University announcing the historic partnership among many leading organizations to create the Freedom Corps clearinghouse; and a July 30 6-month anniversary celebration of the USA Freedom Corps in the East Room of the White House and highlighting results.

Chapter VI

[1] Joseph Campbell with Bill Moyers, *The Power of Myth*, ed. Betty Sue Flowers (New York: Doubleday, 1988).

Chapter VII

[1] Dr. Jurgen Kuhlman, "National Service Programs and Proposals," German Armed Forces Institute for Social Research, National Youth Service: A Global Perspective, < http://www.utas.edu.au/docs/ahugo/NCYS/first/1-Germany.html>; "Civic Service Vision," Center for Social Development, George Warren Brown School of Social Work, < http://gwbweb.wustl.edu/csd/service/vision.htm>; "New Challenges for Peace: From

the Global to the Local View," European Bureau for Conscientious Objection, In Co-Operation with the European Youth Centre, Strasbourg, <http://64.233.161.104/search?q=cache:OSkWPJvUp0gJ:www.coe.int/T/E/cultural_co-operation/Youth/st_2003_ebco.doc+zivildienst+germany+alternative+1949&hl=en&gl=us&ct=clnk&cd=7&lr=lang_en&ie=UTF-8>.

[1] "Alternative to Military Service Starts in Taiwan," *Asian Political News*, August 3, 2000, <http://www.findarticles.com/p/articles/mi_m0WDQ/is_2000_August_7/ai_63946984>.

[1] "Alternative Service," Campaigns of War Tax Resistance and Peace Tax, Conference Documents, The NGO Conscience and Peace Tax International, <http://www.cpti.ws/cpti_docs/brett/pgs/5_1.html>.

[1] 1998 Morocco Report, Refusing to Bear Arms: A World Survey of Conscription and Conscientious Objection to Military Service, War Resisters' International, <http://www.wri-irg.org/co/rtba/index.html>.

[1] President Obama's remarks, signing into law the Edward M. Kennedy Serve America Act, April 21, 2009, at http://my.barackobama.com/page/community/post/obamaforamerica/gGxW4m.

[1] "For Baby Boomers-Get Involved," USA Freedom Corps, < http://www.usafreedomcorps.gov/for_volunteers/boomers/index.asp>.

[1] John M. Bridgeland, Robert D. Putnam, and Harris L. Wofford, More to Give: Tapping the Talents of the Baby Boomer, Silent and Greatest Generations, A Report by Civic Enterprises in association with Peter D. Hart Research Associates for the AARP, September 2008.

[1] John M. Bridgeland, John J. DiIulio, Jr., and Karen Burke Morison, *The Silent Epidemic: Perspectives of High School Dropouts*, A Report by Civic Enterprises in Association with Peter D. Hart Research Associates for the Bill and Melinda Gates Foundation, 2006.

[1] Robert Balfanz and John M. Bridgeland, Grad Nation: A Guidebook to Help Communities Tackle the Dropout Crisis, a report by the Everyone Graduates Center and Civic Enterprises for the America's Promise Alliance.

[1] See Washington Times, July 26, 2006, Looking Out for Dropouts, by John M. Bridgeland

[1] "Working with Children with Parents in Prison," *Children's Services Practice Notes*, January 2002, North Carolina Division of Social Services and the Family and Children's Resource Program, University of North Carolina School of Social Work, < http://ssw.unc.edu/fcrp/cspn/vol7_no1.htm>.

[1] http://www.cdc.gov/malaria/

Photos Credits

Cover: Public Doman.

1. White House photo.

2. White House photo.

3. White House photo.

4. White House photo.

5. White House photo.

6. White House photo.

7. White House photo.

8. Franklin D. Roosevelt Presidential Library & Museum. Public Domain.

9. John F. Kennedy Presidential Library & Museum. Public Domain.

10. Lyndon Baines Johnson Library & Museum. Public Domain.

11. Ronald Reagan Presidential Library, National Archives and Records. Public Domain.

12. George Bush Presidential Library and Museum. Public Domain.

13. Credit: John Gillooly/PEI.

14. White House photo.

15. White House photo.

16. White House photo.

17. White House photo.

18. White House photo.

19. White House photo.

20. Credit: Margaret Hallahan.

21. Credit: Garth Stead.

22. Office of Senator Edward M. Kennedy.

23. White House photo.

General References

Adams, John. Edited by Lester J. Cappon. *The Adams-Jefferson Letters: The Complete Correspondence between Thomas Jefferson and Abigail and John Adams.* Chapel Hill: Institute of Early American History and Culture, University of North Carolina, 1959.

Adler, Mortimer. *Aristotle's Ethics: The Theory of Happiness-II.*

Adler, Mortimer. *We Hold These Truths: Understanding the Ideas and Ideals of the Constitution.* New York: Macmillan, 1987.

Anderson, Gordon. *Philosophy of the United States: Life, Liberty, and the Pursuit of Happiness.* St. Paul: Paragon, 2004.

Andrew, John. *Lyndon Johnson and the Great Society.* Chicago: Ivan Dee, 1998.

Aristotle. *Nicomachean Ethics.*

Bennett, William. *Our Sacred Honor: Words of Advice from the Founders in Stories, Letters, Poems, and Speeches.* Nashville: Broadman and Holman, 1997.

Buckley, William F., Jr. *Gratitude: Reflections on What We Owe to Our Country.* New York: Random House, 1990.

Burner, David. *John F. Kennedy and A New Generation.* New York: Pearson/Longman, 2005.

Burns, James MacGregor. *The Three Roosevelts: Patrician Leaders who Transformed America.* New York: Grove Press, 2001.

Califano, Joseph. *The Triumph and Tragedy of Lyndon Johnson: The White House Years.* College Station: Texas A and M, 2000.

DiIulio, John J. & E.J. Dionne. *What's God Got to Do with the American Experiment?* Washington, D.C.: Brookings Institution Press, 2000.

Eck, Diana. *A New Religious America: How a "Christian Country" Has Become the World's Most Religiously Diverse Nation.* New York: HarperCollins, 2001.

Flexner, James Thomas. *Washington: The Indispensable Man.* Boston: Little Brown, 1974.

Franklin, Benjamin. Edited by J.A. Leo Lemay and P.M. Zall. *Benjamin Franklin's Autobiography: An Authoritative Text, Backgrounds, and Criticism.* New York: Norton, 1986.

Greer, Thomas H. *What Roosevelt Thought: The Social and Political Ideas of Franklin D. Roosevelt.* East Lansing, MI: Michigan State, 2000.

Haidt, Jonathan. *The Happiness Hypothesis: Finding Modern Truth in Ancient Wisdom.* New York: Basic, 2006.

Hill, John. *Revolutionary Values for a New Millennium.* Lanham, MD: Lexington, 2000.

Howe, George Frederick. *Chester A. Arthur: A Quarter-Century of Machine Politics.* New York: F. Ungar, 1957.

Jefferson, Thomas. *Life and Liberty: Reflections on the Pursuit of Happiness* (New York: Modern, 2004).

Jones, Howard Mumford. *The Pursuit of Happiness.* Cambridge, MA: Harvard, 1953.

Kass, Amy A.; Leon R. Kass; & Diana Schaub. *What So Proudly We Hail: The American Soul in Story, Speech and Song.* Wilmington, Delaware: ISI Books. 2011

Karabell, Zachary. *Chester Alan Arthur.* New York: Times Books, 2004.

Lama, Dalai and Howard Cutler. *The Art of Happiness: A Handbook for Living.* London: Hodder and Stoughton, 1998.

McCullough, David. *John Adams.* New York: Simon and Schuster, 2001.

McCullough, David. *1776.* New York: Simon and Schuster, 2005.

Morgan, Edmund Sears. *The Meaning of Independence: John Adams, George Washington, and Thomas Jefferson.* Charlottesville: University of Virginia, 2004.

Morris, Edmund. *Theodore Rex.* New York: Modern, 2002.

Putnam, Robert. *Bowling Alone: The Collapse and Revival of American Community.* New York: Simon and Schuster, 2000.

Putnam, Robert & Lewis Feldstein with Don Cohen. *Better Together: Restoring the American Community.* New York: Simon and Schuster, 2003.

Schlesinger, Arthur. *The Age of Roosevelt.* Boston: Houghton Mifflin, 1957.

Smith, Adam. Edited by E.G. West. *The Theory of Moral Sentiments.* Indianapolis: Liberty, 1976.

Sorensen, Theodore. *Kennedy.* New York: Harper and Row, 1965.

Stossel, Scott. *Sarge: The Life and Times of Sargent Shriver.* Washington, D.C.: Smithsonian Books, 2004.

Titlebaum, Peter, Gabrielle Williamson, Corinne Daprano, Janine Baer, and Jayne Brahler. *Annotated History of Service Learning, 1862-2002.* National Service Learning Clearinghouse.

Tocqueville, Alexis de. Democracy in America.

Wilson, James Q. & John J. DiIulio, Jr. *American Government: Institutions and Policies.* Boston: Houghton Mifflin, 2006.

Wofford, Harris. *Of Kennedys and Kings: Making Sense of the Sixties.* Pittsburgh: University of Pittsburgh, 1992.

Yarbrough, Jean. *American Virtues: Thomas Jefferson on the Character of a Free People.* Lawrence, KS: University Press of Kansas, 1998

00197366

DATE DUE

PRINTED IN U.S.A.

13927490R00147

Made in the USA
Charleston, SC
09 August 2012